Which? Books are commissioned and published by Which? Ltd,
2 Marylebone Road, London NW1 4DF
Email: books@which.co.uk

British Library Cataloguing in Publication Data
A catalogue record for this book is available from the British Library

ISBN 978 1 84490 143 2

1 3 5 7 9 10 8 6 4 2

Consultant editor: Lynn Wright
Project manager: Emma Callery
Designer: Blanche Williams, Harper Williams Ltd
Proofreader: Kathy Steer
Indexer: Christine Bernstein
Printed and bound by Charterhouse, Hatfield
Distributed by Littlehampton Book Services Ltd, Faraday Close, Durrington, Worthing, West Sussex BN13 3RB

Essential Velvet is an elemental chlorine-free paper produced at Condat in Périgord, France using timber from sustainably managed forests. The mill is ISO14001 and EMAS certified.

For a full list of Which? Books, please call 01903 828557 or access our website at www.which.co.uk, or write to Littlehampton Book Services.

Microsoft®
Excel
2010
made easy

Contents

Get Started

Worksheets and cells

Formulas and functions

Photos and graphics

View and analyse data

Resources

Editorial note

The instructions in this guide refer to the Windows 7 operating system and Microsoft Office Home and Student 2010.

Screenshots are used for illustrative purposes only.

Windows 7 and Microsoft Office Home and Student 2010 are American products. All spellings on the screenshots and on the buttons and boxes in the text are therefore spelled in US English. The rest of the text remains in UK English.

All technical words in the book are either discussed in jargon busters within the text and/or can be found in the Jargon Buster section on pages 153-5.

When asked to click on something, note that this means a left click unless specified otherwise.

Introduction

Introduction

Part of Microsoft's Office suite, Excel is the world's most popular spreadsheet program for both business and home use. It lets you store, organise and analyse information, create budgets and reports, manage inventories and produce calendars, and much more.

Excel 2010 Made Easy covers all the techniques you need to create, edit, format and print your own spreadsheets. Beginning with basic steps that get you started with Excel and become familiar with its interface and features, this book steers you through the process of formatting and organising information, along with using formulas and functions to perform basic and more advanced calculations.

You'll also discover how to jazz up your spreadsheets with photos and graphics. Learn how to add and edit images, work with shapes and special effects such as WordArt, and understand the power of SmartArt graphics.

When you're ready for more advanced tutorials, this book will show you how to use Excel's powerful tools for data analysis. From sorting and filtering data, to charts, tables and pivot tables, you'll learn how to quickly sift through large amounts of data to find the answers you need.

Excel 2010 Made Easy includes a handy guide to Excel's keyboard shortcuts as well as a comprehensive jargon buster that explains technical terms in plain English. Now that you're ready to make the most of Excel, it's time to get started.

Get started

By reading this chapter you'll get to grips with:

- Opening new and existing spreadsheets
- Working with the Ribbon
- Using and creating templates

Excel explained

Part of Microsoft's Office suite, Excel 2010 is a spreadsheet program that uses a grid of columns and rows so you can store, organise, and analyse information. It can perform a wide range of calculations on numeric data – making it ideal for managing home finances. It can also be used to create a wide range of graphs and charts, or even act as a simple database program to store, search and retrieve information such as names and addresses. Here is the Excel interface showing a typical spreadsheet used for a household budget.

Quick access toolbar This provides quick access to common commands such as Save, Undo and Repeat, no matter which Ribbon tab you're in. You can add your own commands. See pages 10-11 for how to do this.

Ribbon On the Ribbon's multiple tabs, you'll find the commands you need to complete everyday tasks. You can add your own tabs that contain your favourite commands. Some groups of commands have an arrow in the bottom right corner, which you can click on to see more options. You can customise the Ribbon to suit your own needs. See pages 12-13 for how to do this.

Row A row is a group of cells that runs across the worksheet from left to right.

Worksheet By default, an Excel workbook contains three work-sheets (also known as spread-sheets). Clicking on the tab will bring that worksheet to view. You can also use the scroll buttons on the left to move between worksheets. You can add, delete, reorder and rename worksheets.

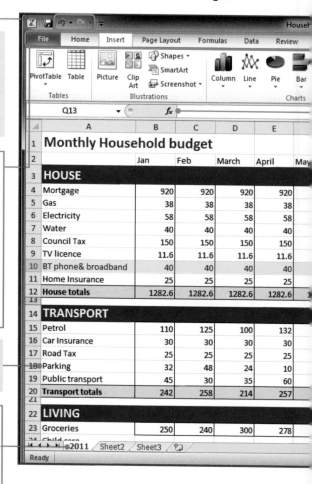

	A	B	C	D	E
1	**Monthly Household budget**				
2		Jan	Feb	March	April	May
3	**HOUSE**				
4	Mortgage	920	920	920	920
5	Gas	38	38	38	38
6	Electricity	58	58	58	58
7	Water	40	40	40	40
8	Council Tax	150	150	150	150
9	TV licence	11.6	11.6	11.6	11.6
10	BT phone& broadband	40	40	40	40
11	Home Insurance	25	25	25	25
12	**House totals**	1282.6	1282.6	1282.6	1282.6
13					
14	**TRANSPORT**				
15	Petrol	110	125	100	132
16	Car Insurance	30	30	30	30
17	Road Tax	25	25	25	25
18	Parking	32	48	24	10
19	Public transport	45	30	35	60
20	**Transport totals**	242	258	214	257
21					
22	**LIVING**				
23	Groceries	250	240	300	278

2011 / Sheet2 / Sheet3

Ready

Formula bar
The formula bar allows you to make mathematical calculations using the data you've entered in the cells of your spreadsheet.

Column
A column is a group of cells that run vertically from the top to the bottom of the worksheet.

Cell On the worksheet grid each rectangle at the intersection of a row and a column is called a cell. A cell's location is given by the letter of the column followed by the number of the intersecting row, for example, the intersection of column L and row 5 is cell L5.

Microsoft Excel non-commercial use

Line
Column
Win/Loss
Sparklines

Slicer
Filter

Hyperlink
Links

A
Text Box

Header & Footer

WordArt
Signature Line
Object
Text

Equation
Symbol
Symbols

tter Other Charts

Horizontal scroll bar
If you have more data in a worksheet than you can view on screen, click and drag the horizontal scroll bar to the left or right to see a particular part of the worksheet.

	H	I	J	K	L	M	N	O	P
	July	Aug	Sep	Oct	Nov	Dec			
920	920	920	920	920	920	920			
38	38	38	38	38	38	38			
58	58	58	58	58	58	58			
40	40	40	40	40	40	40			
150	150	150	150	150	150	150			
11.6	11.6	11.6	11.6	11.6	11.6	11.6			
40	40	40	40	40	40	40			
25	25	25	25	25	25	25			
282.6	1282.6	1282.6	1282.6	1282.6	1282.6	1282.6			
103	78	145	95	120	80	90			
30	30	30	30	30	30	30			
25	25	25	25	25	25	25			
24	22	26	34	10	28	30			
56	34	32	48	42	25	40			
238	189	258	232	227	188	215			
320	298	324	369	270	295	324			

100%

Zoom Click and drag on the slider to zoom in and out of a worksheet.

Page views You have three ways to view your worksheets:
■ **Normal** shows an unlimited number of cells and columns. This is selected by default.
■ **Page Layout** separates the worksheet into pages.
■ **Page Break** shows an overview of the worksheet – useful for adding page breaks.

The Ribbon

The Ribbon that appears at the top of your window has nearly all the commands you need to work in Excel. It contains multiple tabs, each with several related groups of commands. Some groups have an arrow in the bottom-right corner. When you click the arrow, a dialog box launches providing access to additional commands.

The Home tab

This houses the basic formatting tools. From here, you can change the style, size, colour and alignment of your cell content and more. Find out how to use these on pages 36-41.

The Insert tab

From here you can create tables, charts and sparkline graphics from your data (see pages 139-50). You can also add headers and footers, photos and clipart and more (see pages 29 and 88-96).

The Page Layout tab

Here you can set page margins and breaks and specify print areas or repeat rows (see pages 26-9).

The Formulas tab

This holds the Functions Library where you can find a huge array of functions (see pages 66-80). You can also troubleshoot formulas from here.

The Data tab

From here you can perform what-if analysis and import, sort and filter data (see pages 81-3 and 116-29).

The Review tab

Check the contents of your worksheet using the spellchecker (see pages 24-5). You can also review and revise changes to your worksheet and protect it before sharing with others (see page 30).

The View tab

Zoom in and out of a worksheet to make it easier to view. You can switch between worksheet views or active workbooks, arrange windows, freeze panes and more (see pages 112-15).

Tip

Along with the seven main tabs, further contextual tool tabs appear on the Ribbon, depending on your actions in Excel. For example, if you click in a table, two extra Table Tools tabs appear – one for Design and one for Layout. These contain the controls you need to format items. Similar contextual tab tools appear if you click on a picture, edit a header or footer, or click in a text box.

Customise the Ribbon

You can customise the Ribbon by creating new tabs to house the commands you use most often. Commands are kept within a group, and you can create as many groups as you need to keep your tab organised. You can also add commands to any of the default tabs, provided you create a custom group in the tab.

1 Right click the Ribbon and select **Customize the Ribbon...**.

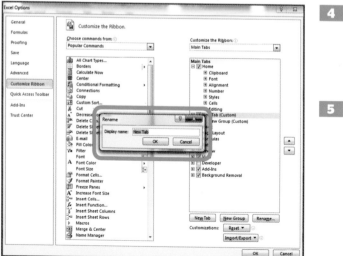

2 In the dialog box that appears, click **New Tab**. A new tab will be created with a new group inside it. (Alternatively, to add a new group to an existing tab, select the tab and then click **New Group**).

3 Click on the new tab and then **Rename...**.

4 In the 'Rename' dialog box that appears, give the new tab a more descriptive name.

5 Under the new renamed tab, click the **New Group (Custom)**.

6 Select a command from the list on the left (in this case, 'Right Arrow'), then click **Add >>**. You can also drag commands directly into a group.

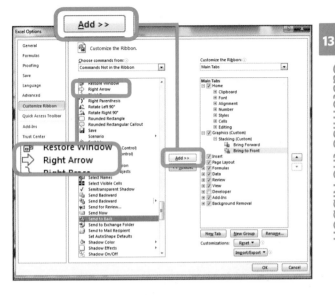

7 If you can't see the command you want, click on the 'Choose commands from' **drop-down arrow** above the list, and click **All Commands**.

8 Use the arrow keys to order your commands exactly the way you want them to appear on the Ribbon tab. In this case, up means left and down means right.

9 When you have finished adding commands, click **OK**.

Shrink the Ribbon

If you find that the Ribbon is taking up too much screen space you can choose to minimise it:

1 Click the arrow in the upper-right corner of the Ribbon to minimise it.

2 To maximise the Ribbon, click the arrow again.

> When the Ribbon is minimised, you can make it reappear by clicking on a tab. However, the Ribbon will disappear again when you're not using it.

The Backstage view and Quick Access Toolbar

Along with the Ribbon (see pages 10–11), the Backstage view and the Quick Access Toolbar hold the commands you need for common tasks in Excel.

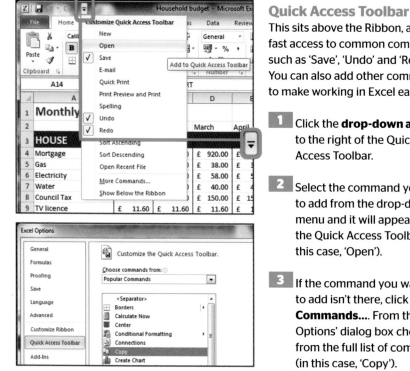

Backstage view

Here you'll find various options for opening, saving, printing or sharing a document. To get to the Backstage view:

1 With an Excel 2010 file open, click the **File** tab.

2 Choose an option on the left side of the page, such as **Info**.

3 To return to your document, click any tab on the Ribbon.

Quick Access Toolbar

This sits above the Ribbon, and offers fast access to common commands such as 'Save', 'Undo' and 'Repeat'. You can also add other commands to make working in Excel easier.

1 Click the **drop-down arrow** to the right of the Quick Access Toolbar.

2 Select the command you want to add from the drop-down menu and it will appear in the Quick Access Toolbar (in this case, 'Open').

3 If the command you want to add isn't there, click **More Commands....** From the 'Excel Options' dialog box choose from the full list of commands (in this case, 'Copy').

Open an Excel workbook

An Excel file is called a workbook and each one contains several worksheets (spreadsheets).

Create a new, blank workbook

 Click the **File** tab to see the Backstage view.

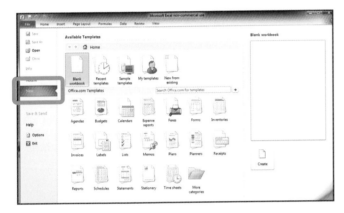

2 Click **New**.

3 Select **Blank** workbook under 'Available Templates'.

4 Click **Create**. A new, blank workbook appears to the right in the Excel window.

Open an existing workbook

1 Click the **File** tab to see the Backstage view.

2 Click **Open**. Select a workbook (in this case, 'Household budget') and click **Open**.

3 If you've opened an Excel workbook recently, you can access it in the 'Recent' list. Click on the **File** tab and select **Recent**.

Open Excel 97-2003 workbooks

As both programs share the same XML-based file format, workbooks created in Excel 2007 will open as normal in Excel 2010. However, when you open a workbook that was created in Excel 97-2003, it will open in 'compatibility mode'. This is indicated by the words '[Compatibility Mode]' that follow the document name in the title bar.

Working in compatibility mode disables Excel 2010's new features and saves the workbook in the Excel 97-2003 file format (.xls) so that it can be still edited in earlier versions of Excel. If the title bar doesn't include the words '[Compatibility Mode]', the workbook is in Excel 2010 mode and all features are available.

You can choose to work and save a document in compatibility mode or convert it to Excel 2010's .xlsx format. By converting the document, you gain full access to Excel 2010's new features, but after the workbook is converted, it is no longer available in the original file format.

Convert a workbook to Excel 2010 mode

1 With the workbook open, click the **File** tab.

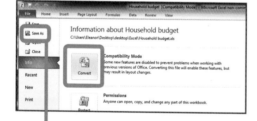

2 If you want to convert the workbook without saving a copy, click **Info** and then click **Convert**.

3 A dialog box may appear with a message about converting workbooks. If so, click **OK**.

4 To work in the current file format, click **Yes** to close and reopen the workbook.

Save As Instead of converting, you can save a copy of the workbook in Excel 2010 file format. That way, the workbook is preserved in the original format. At Step 2, click **Save As**, give the workbook a name in the 'File name' box, and select '.xlsx' in the 'Save as type' list. Then click **Save**.

Check a workbook for compatibility with older versions of Excel

If you're saving an Excel 2010 workbook as an .xls file so that it can be opened in earlier versions of Excel, it's a good idea to run the Compatibility Checker. This checks for potential compatibility issues, such as missing features, and suggests ways to resolve them.

1 With the workbook you want to check open, click the **File** tab and then **Info**.

2 Click **Check for Issues**, and then click **Check Compatibility**.

3 To check for compatibility every time you save the workbook, select the 'Check compatibility when saving this workbook' check box.

4 To create a report of all the issues that are listed in the 'Summary' box, click **Copy to New Sheet**.

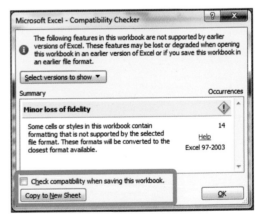

Tip

The Compatibility Checker may offer one or more of the following options in the Summary box. They will be coloured blue and underlined. Click **Find** to see exactly where the issues are located in the worksheet; click **Fix** to resolve simple issues; or click **Help** for more information on the nature of the incompatibility.

Jargon buster

File format Refers to the specific way that information is stored within a computer file. The letters that appear after the file name show what type of file it is and what type of program will open it – for example, a Microsoft Excel file ends in .xlsx.

Use a template

Excel has many templates that can save you time and effort. These pre-designed spreadsheets come with ready-made formatting and predefined formulas – so you don't need to worry about performing calculations and writing your own formulas.

Create a new workbook using a template

1 Click the **File** tab to go to Backstage view.

2 Select **New**. The 'Available Templates' pane appears.

3 Click **Sample templates** to choose a built-in template or select an 'Office.com Templates' category to choose a template from Microsoft's website.

4 Thumbnail images of the templates can be seen in the centre. Click on one of these to see a larger preview on the right.

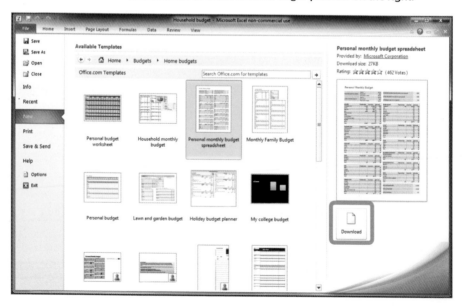

5 Click a template and then click **Create**. If using an Office.com template, 'Create' will be replaced by **Download**.

6 A new workbook will appear using your selected template.

Create your own template

When you can't find a template that suits your needs, you can create your own – either by making changes to an existing template or by using an Excel 2010 document you've already created and formatted as shown here.

1 Click the **File** tab and then **Open**. Select the workbook that you want to use as a template.

2 Check – and change if necessary – the workbook settings such as text, data, formatting, formulas and graphics to suit your template.

3 Remove any text or data that doesn't need to be in the template. Only text or data that you want to appear in all workbooks based on that template should be left.

4 Click the **File** tab and select **Save As**.

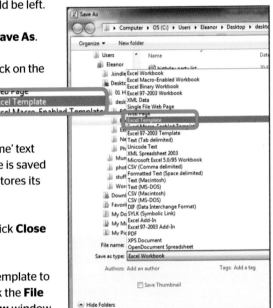

5 In the 'Save As' dialog box, click on the 'Save as type' **drop-down arrow** and select **Excel Template**.

6 Type a name into the 'File Name' text box. Click **Save**. The template is saved to the location where Word stores its document templates.

7 Click the **File** tab and then click **Close** to close the template.

8 When you want to use this template to create a new workbook, click the **File** tab and select it from the **New** window.

Tip

If you want to create a new workbook using an existing Excel workbook as a template, there's a quick and easy way to do this. Click the **File** tab and click **New**. Select **New from Existing** in the main panel and then choose an Excel workbook to use as a template. Click **Open**. A new, untitled file will open but all the text, data and formatting from the workbook you have selected as a template will appear in this new workbook. The original Excel workbook remains untouched.

Save an Excel workbook

Excel has two commands that let you save your workbook – which one you use depends on whether you're saving for the first time or saving a file you have previously saved.

Use Save As command

This lets you choose a name for your workbook and the location where it will be stored. Use this when saving a workbook for the first time (even if you select 'Save', the 'Save As' dialog box will appear) or if you want to save a different version of a workbook while keeping the original.

1 Click **File** to open the Backstage view.

2 Click **Save As**.
In the 'Save As' dialog box, choose where to save your workbook by selecting a folder from the left-hand pane.

3 Type in a name for the workbook. Here, it's 'Household budget'.

4 Click **Save**.

Use the Save Command

To save your workbook with same name and location, use the 'Save' command. Do this regularly as you work to ensure your data is safe should something unexpected like a computer crash happen.

1 Click **Save** on the Quick Access Toolbar.

2 Your workbook is saved.

Save as an older format

Excel 2010 workbooks are saved in the .xlsx file format, which means you can share them with anyone using Excel 2010 or 2007. Earlier versions of Excel, however, use a different file format, so to open your spreadsheet in these versions, you must save it as an Excel 97-2003 workbook.

 Click **File** to open the Backstage view.

2 Select **Save As**.

3 In the 'Save As type' drop-down menu, select **Excel 97-2003 Workbook**.

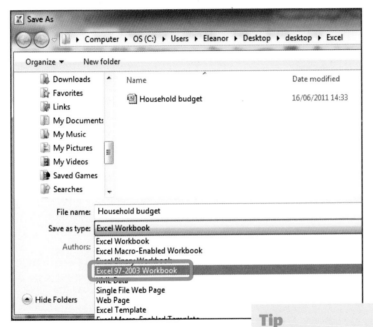

4 Choose a location for the saved file.

5 Type in a name for your workbook.

6 Click **Save**.

Tip
You can also save your Excel 2010 workbook in a different file format so that it can be opened in another software program. In the 'Save As' dialog box, click on the 'Save as type' **drop-down arrow** and select a file type from the list. Excel supports a wide range of file formats but those available here will depend on the type of sheet that's active (a worksheet, chart sheet or other type of sheet).

Enable Excel's autosave feature

Excel automatically saves your active workbook to a temporary location at regular intervals using its AutoRecover feature, so should something unexpected happen such as a power cut or you accidently close a workbook without first saving it, a version of your file will be saved.

Enable AutoRecover

1 With the workbook open, click the **File** tab and, under 'Help', click **Options**.

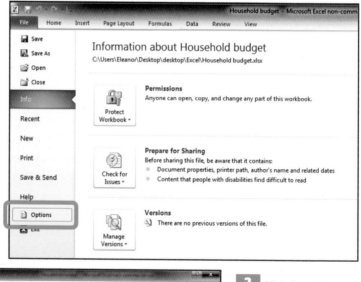

2 Click **Save** from the left-hand pane.

3 Tick the **Save AutoRecover information every 10 minutes** check box.

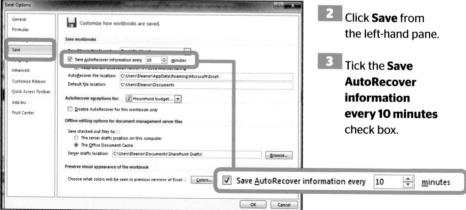

4 In the 'minutes' field, you can specify how often you want the program to save your document.

5 Select the **Keep the last autosaved version if I close without saving** check box.

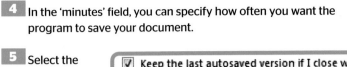

☑ Keep the last autosaved version if I close without saving

6 Click **OK**.

Open an autosaved version of your workbook

1 Open a workbook that was previously closed without saving.

2 Click **File** to get to the Backstage view.

3 In Backstage view, click **Info**.

4 If there are autosaved versions of your workbook, they will appear under 'Versions'. Click on the file to open it.

5 You will see a yellow caution note on the workbook ribbon. To use this version of the workbook click **Restore** and then click **OK**.

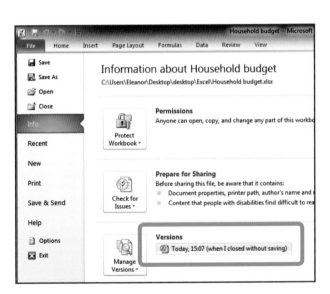

Excel autosaves every 10 minutes by default, although you can change this for more frequent autosaves. If you're working for less than this (or the number of minutes specified), Excel will not autosave.

Tip

If you're looking for an autosaved version of a file that has no previously saved versions, browse all autosaved files by clicking on the **Manage Versions** button and selecting **Recover Unsaved Workbooks** from the drop-down menu.

Enable Excel's autosave feature

Get started

Check spelling in your workbook

Don't let silly spelling errors ruin your carefully crafted spreadsheet – use Excel's spellchecker to clear them up. It checks for mistakes only in the open worksheet. To check multiple worksheets in your workbook, select them first before you run the spellchecker. You can also check just part of a worksheet – simply select the cells first.

1 With the workbook open, click the **Review** tab, then in the 'Proofing' group click **Spelling**.

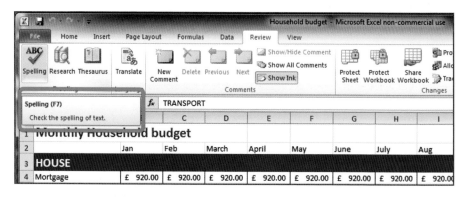

2 Excel checks the spelling of text entries in your selection. When it sees a potential mistake, it displays the 'Spelling' dialog box.

3 In the dialog box, Excel offers one or more suggested replacements for the error. Click on a suggestion and then click **Change** to use it as a replacement for the original word. Click **Change All** to change all occurrences of the original word to the new word in the Suggestions list box.

4 If no suggestion is given, or the correct replacement isn't shown, you can type in a new spelling in the 'Not in Dictionary' box.

5 When finished, you'll see a dialog box saying 'The spelling check is complete for the selected cells'. Click **OK**.

Choose to ignore errors

Excel's spellchecker is not always accurate. It may flag words – such as people's names or place names – as potential spelling mistakes even if they're correct. In this case, you can choose to leave it as it was originally written by selecting one of the following:

- **Ignore Once:** skips this instance of the word without changing it.
- **Ignore All:** skips this word without changing it, and skips all subsequent appearances of this word in the worksheet.
- **Add to Dictionary:** this adds the word to the dictionary so that it's never flagged as an error in subsequent spell checks.

Change the spell check language

Excel 2010 may spell check your text using a US English dictionary by default, but you can change the language used for spell checking.

1 With the workbook open, click the **File** tab and, under 'Help', click **Options**.

2 Click **Proofing** in the left-hand pane.

3 Click the 'Dictionary language' **drop-down arrow** and select the language to use. In this case, **English (U.K.)**.

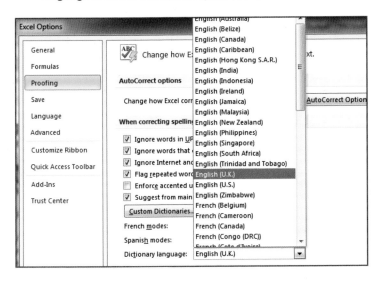

4 Click **OK**. When you run a spell check, it will check in the language you have selected, which is now the default language.

Print an Excel document

In Excel you can preview and print selected worksheets from the Print pane. To open this, click the **File** tab to see the Backstage view, then click **Print**. The 'Print' pane appears, with the print settings on the left and a preview of your worksheets on the right.

Print a worksheet

1 Select the worksheet you wish to print. To print more than one worksheet, click on the first worksheet tab, then while holding down the Ctrl key, click on the other worksheet tabs.

2 Click the **File** tab to go to the Backstage view.

3 Click **Print** to access the 'Print' pane.

4 Under 'Settings', click on **Print Selection** and then on **Print Active Sheets** from the drop-down menu.

5 Click **Print**.

Print a selection

You can choose to print just part of a worksheet – specific rows or columns. Here's how:

1 Select the cells that you want to print. Click the **File** tab to go to the Backstage view.

2 Click **Print** to access the 'Print' pane.

3 Under 'Settings', click on **Print Selection** and then on **Print Selection** from the drop-down menu.

4 Click **Print**.

Change page orientation

Depending on the structure of your Excel spreadsheet – how many rows and columns it has – you may want to change the page orientation to fit more on the page when printed. Selecting 'Portrait' will orient the page vertically and 'Landscape' will orient the page horizontally.

BE CAREFUL!

Resizing a worksheet so that it can fit on one page may seem a good idea, but if it is scaled too small it could be difficult to read.

1 Click the **File** tab to see the Backstage view.

2 Click **Print** to access the 'Print' pane.

3 Under 'Settings', click on **Orientation** and then on **Portrait Orientation** or **Landscape Orientation** from the drop-down menu. The page orientation will change and you can see this in the preview pane.

Fit a worksheet on one page

1 Click the **File** tab to see the Backstage view.

2 Click **Print** to access the 'Print' pane.

3 Under 'Settings', click on **Scaling** and then on **Fit Sheet on One Page** from the drop-down menu.

4 The worksheet will be reduced in size until it fits on one page.

Print row and column headers on every page

If you need to print your worksheet on several pages, you can make it easier to read if you use Excel's 'Print Titles' feature to print row and column headers on every page.

1 Click the worksheet that you want to print with row and column headings.

2 Click the **Page Layout** tab.

Page Setup

| Page | Margins | Header/Footer | **Sheet** |

Print area:

Print titles

Rows to repeat at top:

Columns to repeat at left:

Print

☐ Gridlines
☐ Black and white
☐ Draft quality
☑ Row and column headings

Comments: (None)

Cell errors as: displayed

Page order

◉ Down, then over
○ Over, then down

Print...   Print Preview   Options...

OK   Cancel

3 In the 'Page Setup' group, click **Print Titles**.

4 The 'Page Setup' dialog box appears. Click the icon at the end of the 'Rows to repeat at top' field.

5 Your cursor becomes the small selection arrow. Click on the rows you want to appear on each printed page. The 'Rows to repeat at top' dialog box will record your selection.

6 Click the icon at the end of the 'Rows to repeat at top' field to record your selection. Repeat for 'Columns to repeat at left', if necessary.

7 Click **OK**. Click the **Print Preview** button to open the 'Print' pane to see a preview of how each page will look when printed.

Tip

To see how the changes you make will affect how your worksheet will print, click the **Print Preview** button in the 'Page Setup' dialog box.

Set print margins

Print margins are the blank areas between the worksheet data and the edges of the printed page. To make sure your worksheet is well positioned on a printed page, you can use Excel's predefined margins or create your own custom margins, or centre the worksheet horizontally or vertically on the page.

1 Select the worksheet that you want to print.

2 On the **Page Layout** tab, in the 'Page Setup' group, click **Margins**.

3 From the drop-down list click **Normal**, **Wide** or **Narrow** to use one of the predefined settings.

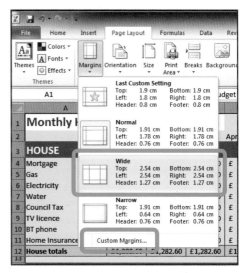

4 To create custom page margins, click **Custom Margins...** from the drop-down menu. In the 'Page Setup' dialog box, then enter the margin sizes that you want in the 'Top', 'Bottom', 'Left' and 'Right' boxes.

5 You can centre horizontally or vertically. Under 'Center on page', tick either or both **Horizontally** or **Vertically**. You can also set header or footer margins, by entering values in the 'Header' or 'Footer' boxes.

6 Click **OK**.

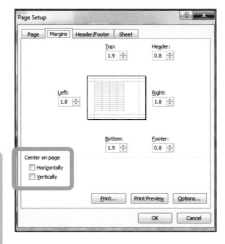

If you have more than one worksheet in your workbook, you can choose to print either the whole workbook or specific worksheets as indicated by the 'Print Active Sheets' option. A worksheet is considered active if it's selected.

Protect your workbook

If you are ready to share your workbook with others but want to stop them from making changes to it, you can use Excel's straight forward protection options to safeguard your file. There are several layers of protection available from simple read-only restrictions to applying a digital signature.

1 With your workbook open, click the **File** tab.

2 In the Backstage view, click **Info**.

3 In 'Permissions', click **Protect Workbook**. Then choose from the following options:

- **Mark as Final:** makes the workbook read-only, so no changes or additions can be made.
- **Encrypt with Password:** lets you set a password so that only those who have the password can open the workbook.
- **Protect Current Sheet:** lets you set a password and restrict permission for users to select, sort or edit areas of a worksheet.
- **Protect Workbook Structure:** lets you set password protection and options to stop users from changing, moving or deleting important data.
- **Add a Digital Signature:** adds a visible or invisible digital signature.

If you have a Microsoft Live ID, you'll see a further option in Step 3 called 'Restrict Permission by People'. This uses Microsoft's IRM (Information Right Management) Service to restrict or assign permission to certain users.

Jargon buster

Digital signature An electronic, encrypted, stamp of authentication used on digital files such as documents or email messages. A digital signature confirms that the file originated from the signer and has not been altered.

Worksheets and cells

By reading this chapter you'll get to grips with:

- Moving, naming and working with worksheets
- Modifying columns and rows
- Adding and formatting cells content

Worksheets and cells

Get started with worksheets

When you open an Excel workbook, you will see it consists of three worksheets with the default names of Sheet1, Sheet2 and Sheet3. Look at the bottom of the window, just above the Status bar to see the worksheet tabs. You can rename worksheets, and add, move, copy or delete worksheets. You may, for example, wish to create a household finance workbook that consists of 12 worksheets – one for each month – or a worksheet for each year.

	A	B	C	D
1	**Monthly Household budget**			
2		Jan	Feb	March
3	**HOUSE**			
4	Mortgage	920	920	920
5	Gas	38	38	38
6	Electricity	58	58	58
7	Water	40	40	40
8	Council Tax	150	150	150
9	TV licence	11.6	11.6	11.6
10	BT phone& broadband	40	40	40
11	Home Insurance	25	25	25
12	**House totals**	1282.6	1282.6	1282.6
14	**TRANSPO**			
15	Petrol		125	100
16	Car Insuran		30	30
17	Road Tax		25	25
18	Parking		48	24
19	Public transp		30	35
20	**Transport tot**		258	214
22	**LIVING**			
23	Groceries		240	300

Pop-up menu: Insert..., Delete..., Rename, Move or Copy..., View Code, Protect Sheet..., Tab Color, Hide, Unhide..., Select All Sheets

Tabs: 2011, Sheet2, Sheet3, Sheet1

Rename a worksheet

1 Right click the worksheet tab you want to rename.

2 On the pop-up menu, click **Rename**.

Rename

3 The text on the worksheet tab will now be highlighted in black. Type a name for your worksheet.

4 Click anywhere outside of the tab to apply the new name.

Add a new worksheet

1 Click on the **Insert Worksheet** icon that can be found to the right of the worksheet tabs.

19	Public transport	4	30	35
20	**Transport totals**	242	258	214
22	**LIVING**			
23	Groceries	250	240	300

Tabs: 2011, Sheet2, Sheet3

Ready

2 A new worksheet will appear.

1 Right click the tab of the worksheet you want to move or copy.

2 From the worksheet menu click **Move or Copy...**.

12	House totals	1282.0	1282.0	1282.0	1282.0	1282.0	1282.0	128
13								
14	**TRANSPO**							
15	Petrol		125	100	132	140	103	
16	Car Insuran		30	30	30	30	30	
17	Road Tax		25	25	25	25	25	
18	Parking		48	24	10	18	24	
19	Public transp		30	35	60	48	56	
20	**Transport to**		258	214	257	261	238	1
21								
22	**LIVING**							
23	Groceries		240	300	278	255	320	2

Worksheet menu:
- Insert...
- Delete
- Rename
- Move or Copy...
- View Code
- Protect Sheet...
- Tab Color ▶
- Hide
- Unhide...
- Select All Sheets

Tabs: **2011** Sheet2 Sheet3 Sheet1

Ready

3 In the 'Move or Copy' dialog box, tick the **Create a copy** box if you want to copy the worksheet or leave blank if you just want to move the selected sheet.

4 Select a location for the worksheet in the 'Before sheet' pane.

5 Click **OK**. Your worksheet will appear in the new location. If you selected 'Create a copy' (see Step 3), your worksheet will be copied with the same name as the original worksheet, but the title shows a version number, such as 2012 (2).

Move or Copy dialog box:

Move selected sheets

To book:
Household budget.xlsx

Before sheet:
2011
Sheet2
Sheet3
Sheet1
(move to end)

☑ Create a copy

OK   Cancel

Delete a worksheet

1 Right click the tab of the worksheet you want to delete.

2 On the pop-up menu, click **Delete**.

11	Home Insurance	25	25	25	25	25
12	**House totals**	1282.6	1282.6	1282.6	1282.6	1282.6
13						
14	**TRANSPORT**					
15	Petrol	110	125	1		
16	Car Insurance	30	30			
17	Road Tax	25	25			
18	Parking	32	48			
19	Public transport	45	30			
20	**Transport totals**	242	258	2		
21						
22	**LIVING**					
23	Groceries	250	240	3		
24	Child care					

Insert...

Delete

Rename

Move or Copy...

View Code

Protect Sheet...

Tab Color ▶

Hide

Unhide...

Select All Sheets

| 2011 | Sheet2 | Sheet3 | Sheet1 | **2011 (2)** |

Ready

3 The worksheet will be deleted from your workbook.

Colour worksheet tabs

Changing the colour of individual worksheet tabs can help you organise your workbook.

1 Right click the worksheet tab you want to colour.

2 On the pop-up menu, click **Tab Color**.

3 From the drop-down menu, select a colour.

4 Click anywhere outside the tab to see the new tab colour applied.

Tip
You can also move a worksheet using drag and drop. Click the tab of the worksheet you want to move. The mouse will change to show a small worksheet icon. Drag the worksheet tab to its new location and release your mouse.

Group and ungroup worksheets

The quickest way to make the same changes or add the same data to more than one worksheet in a workbook, is to first group them. When you group worksheets, any changes made to one worksheet will be made to every worksheet in the group. For example, you can:

- Add or edit data on all the worksheets at once.
- Apply formatting to a same selection on all of the worksheets at the same time.
- Insert headers and footers.
- Move, copy or delete a group of worksheets.
- Print a selection of sheets at the same time.

> If you've grouped only some of the worksheets in your workbook, you can quickly ungroup them by clicking on a worksheet tab that's not in the group.

Group worksheets

1 Select the first worksheet you want in the group.

2 Hold down the **Ctrl** key on your keyboard and click on the tab of the next worksheet you want in the group. Continue until all of the worksheets you want to group are selected.

3 Release the Ctrl key to group the worksheets. The worksheet tabs appear white to show they are grouped.

Ungroup worksheets

1 Right click one of the worksheets.

2 From the pop-up menu click **Ungroup Sheets**. The worksheets will be ungrouped.

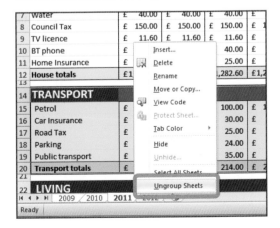

Work with cells

Cells are the core building blocks of an Excel worksheet, but you need to know how to work with cells and cell content before moving on to perform calculations or data analysis.

Each cell in a workbook can have its own content such as:

▪ **Text:** letters, numbers and dates.
▪ **Formatting:** attributes that change the way cell content is displayed. For example, text can be made bold or italic.
▪ **Formulas and Functions:** these calculate cell values. For example, *SUM(cell A1, cell A2 ...)* is a formula that adds the values of multiple cells.
▪ **Comments:** each cell can contain comments from more than one reviewer.

Select a cell

1 Click on a cell to select it.

2 When a cell is selected its border appears bold, and the row and column headings are highlighted.

3 The cell will stay selected until you click on another cell in the worksheet.

4 To select more than one cell, click and drag your mouse across adjoining cells to highlight them. Release the mouse. The cells remain selected until you click on another cell in the worksheet.

Tip
You can navigate through your worksheet cell by cell, either vertically or horizontally, by using your keyboard's arrow keys. You can also press **Tab** on your keyboard to move forward to the next cell or **Enter** to move vertically.

Add content to a cell

1 Select a cell.

2 Type content directly into the selected cell. It will appear in the cell and in the formula bar.

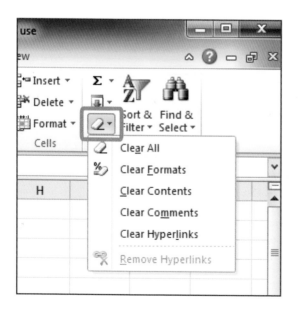

3 You also can enter or edit cell content using the formula bar.

Delete content from a cell

1 Select the cell whose content you wish to delete. On the Ribbon, in the **Home** tab, click the **Clear** icon.

2 From the drop-down menu, click **Clear Contents**.

3 Alternatively, use the keyboard's Backspace key to delete content from a single cell.

Delete cells

Rather than delete content from a cell, you can choose to delete the cell itself. However, when you choose this option, the cells underneath will shift up and replace the deleted cell by default.

1 Select the cell or cells that you want to delete.

2 On the **Home** tab, in the 'Cells' group, click **Delete**.

3 The cell or cells will be deleted and your column content below will shift up to fill the space.

4 By default cells are shifted upwards in a column, but if you prefer to replace a cell with the adjacent cells in the row, click the 'Delete' **drop-down arrow** and then click **Delete Cells**. From the 'Delete' dialog box, choose your preferred option (in this case, 'Shift cells left') and click **OK**.

Copy content from one cell to another

You can use Excel's copy and paste commands to copy - or cut - content from one cell to another.

 Select the cell or cells you wish to copy.

2 On the Ribbon, click either **Copy** or **Cut**. You'll see the border of the selected cells change in appearance to a dotted line.

3 Select the cell or cells where you want to paste the content. On the Ribbon, click **Paste**. The content will then appear in the highlighted cells.

Copy content using the fill handle

You can use the fill handle to copy cell content from one cell to another. You can drag the fill handles either vertically or horizontally.

1 Select the cell or cells with the content you want to use.

2 Move your cursor over the fill handle – the white cross will become a black cross.

3 Click and drag the fill handle until all the cells you want to fill are highlighted.

4 Release the mouse and the cells will be filled.

Herts Lawn Bowling Club Shop – Microsoft Excel non-commercial use						
Formulas	Data	Review	View			

=1<50,5,0)

Club Shop

	B	C	D	E	F	G
	ITEM NUMBER	PRICE	VAT	TOTAL	SURCHARGE	
	AWT123	£40.99	£8.20	£49.19	£5.00	£5.00
	AGT234	£48.99	£9.80	£58.79	£0.00	£0.00
	BLZ765	£40.99	£8.20	£49.19	£5.00	£5.00
	BLZ236	£40.99	£8.20	£49.19	£0.00	£5.00
	LWT987	£30.99	£6.20	£37.19	£5.00	£5.00
	LGT765	£28.99	£5.80	£34.79	£5.00	£5.00
	UVP675	£21.99	£4.40	£26.39	£5.00	£5.00
	UWJ239	£49.99	£10.00	£59.99	£5.00	£5.00
	SSB779	£12.99	£2.60	£15.59	£5.00	£5.00
	LWT569	£17.99	£3.60	£21.59	£0.00	£5.00
	UPS453	£9.99	£2.00	£11.99	£5.00	£5.00
	BB3498	£59.99	£12.00	£71.99	£5.00	£5.0
				£485.86		

Jargon buster

Fill handle A small black dot or square in the bottom right corner of the active cell that can be used to copy a cell's contents to adjacent cells.

Move cells by dragging and dropping

1 Select the cells you wish to move.

2 Position your mouse on one of the outside edges of the selected cells. The mouse changes from a white cross to a black cross with four arrows.

3 Click and drag the cells to the new location.

4 Release your mouse key and the cells will be dropped there.

Use Excel's Paste Special options

Normally when you copy and paste content into a cell, all the information from that cell is copied across, but you can use Excel's Paste Special feature to choose other options. For example, you may want to copy and paste only the formatting or the formula used in a cell without the actual cell contents.

1 Copy the cell content you wish to use (see pages 40-1).

2 On the **Home** tab, in the 'Clipboard' group, click the 'Paste' **drop-down arrow** and then choose **Paste Special...**.

3 In the 'Paste Special' dialog box (see opposite), choose a 'Paste' option to specify which parts of the selection to use:

- **All:** to paste everything in the cell selection.
- **Formulas:** to paste all the text, numbers and formulas but not the formatting.
- **Values:** to convert formulas and paste their calculated values.
- **Formats:** to paste only the formatting of the selected cells, such as font colour or fill colour but not the cell content.
- **Comments:** to paste only comments attached to the cells.

- **Validation:** to paste only the data validation rules that have been applied to the selected cells.
- **All Using Source theme:** to paste all the information and the cell styles.
- **All except borders:** to paste everything in the cell selection without copying the borders.
- **Column widths:** to paste only column width information.
- **Formulas and number formats:** to include the number formats assigned to the pasted values and formulas.
- **Values and number formats:** to convert formulas to their calculated values and include any number formats assigned to the copied or cut values.
- **All merging conditional formats:** to paste conditional formatting into the cell range.

4 Although **None** is selected by default, you can choose to perform a mathematical calculation when pasting, using the value of the copied cell and that of the target cell. Choose from **Add**, **Subtract**, **Multiply** or **Divide**.

5 At the bottom of the 'Paste Special' dialog box, are further options:

- **Skip blanks:** Excel will paste only from filled cells.
- **Transpose:** to change the orientation of the pasted entries.
- **Paste Link:** to create a link between the copied and pasted content so that changes to the original cells automatically update in the pasted copies.

6 Click **OK** to paste your selection.

Modify cells, columns and rows

When you first open an Excel workbook, you'll see that all the cells are the same default size and it's unlikely that they'll be big enough to display all the text you've entered into them. Fortunately, you can modify cells and adjust column widths and row heights to ensure your content is viewable.

Change column width

1 Move your cursor over the column line in the column heading. The white cross will become a double arrow.

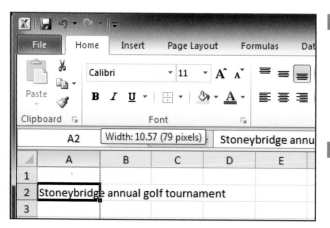

2 Click and drag the column to the right to increase the column width or to the left to decrease the column width.

3 Release the mouse. The column width will change.

Change row height

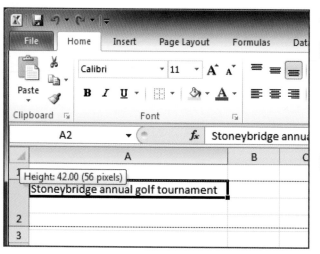

1 Move your cursor over the row line in the row heading. The white cross will become a double arrow.

2 Click and drag the row downwards to increase the row height or upwards to decrease the row height.

 Release the mouse. The row height will change.

Set row height or column width with a specific measurement

1 Select the rows or columns you want to modify.

2 On the **Home** tab, click **Format**.

3 From the drop-down menu, select either **Row Height...** or **Column Width...**.

4 In the respective dialog box that appears, enter a specific measurement for row height or column width.

5 Click **OK**.

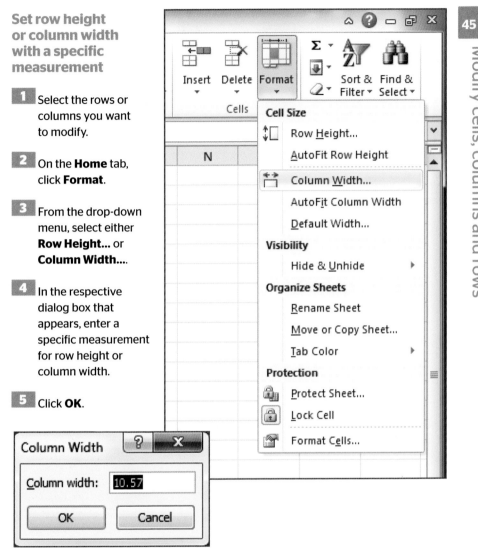

Tip
When you add a column, by default Excel formats it with the same formatting as the column to the left. If you add a row, it formats it with the same formatting as the row above. To see more formatting options, move your cursor over the 'Insert Options' button that appears when you add a new column or row. Select an option from the drop-down menu.

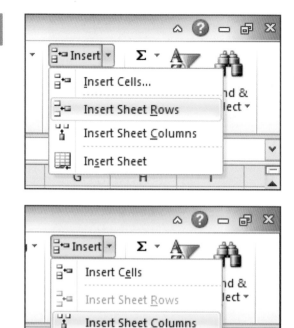

Add rows

1 Select the row below where you want the new row to appear.

2 On the **Home** tab, in the 'Cells' group, click **Insert** and a new row will appear.

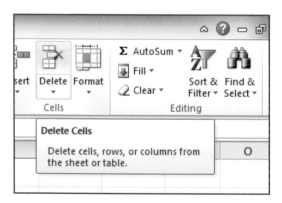

Add columns

1 Select the column to the right of where you want the new column to appear. For example, if you want to insert a column between A and B, select column B.

2 On the **Home** tab, in the 'Cells' group, click **Insert** and a new column will appear.

Delete rows and columns

1 Select the rows or columns you want to delete.

2 On the **Home** tab, click **Delete** and the rows or columns will be deleted.

Make text fit

Often a cell will contain more text than it can display but you don't want to extend the entire column width. You can solve this by either wrapping text within the cells so that it appears on several lines or merging the cell with an empty adjoining cell.

Wrap text

1 Select the cells with text you want to wrap.

2 On the **Home** tab, click **Wrap Text**.

3 The text in the selected cells will be wrapped within the cell, and appear on more than one line.

Merge cells

1 Select the cells you want to merge.

2 On the **Home** tab, click **Merge & Center**. The selected cells will be merged and the text will be centred.

3 For more merge options, click the 'Merge & Center' **drop-down arrow** and then choose an option:
- **Merge & Center:** to merge selected cells into one cell and centre the text.
- **Merge Across:** to merge each row of selected cells into larger cells – useful for merging content across multiple rows of cells without creating one large cell.
- **Merge Cells:** to merge selected cells into one cell.
- **Unmerge Cells:** to unmerge the selected cells.

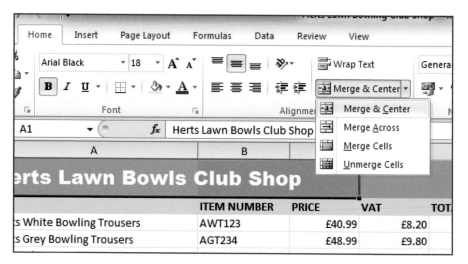

Split merged cells

You can split only cells that were previously merged.

1 Select the merged cell.

2 On the **Home** tab, in the 'Alignment' group, click **Merge & Center**. It will be highlighted yellow.

3 The contents of the merged cell will appear in the upper-left cell of the range of split cells.

Format cells

Changing the colour, size and alignment of your text and applying other formatting to cells and numbers will help make your text and data more readable and easier to understand. Once you've entered text or data into the cells of an Excel worksheet and adjusted columns and row widths, you can then format the cell content.

Change the font

1 Select the cells you want to change.

2 On the **Home** tab, in the 'Font' group, click the current font **drop-down arrow**.

3 On the drop-down menu, move your cursor over a font to see a live preview on your worksheet.

4 Click a font to apply it to the selected cells.

Tip

If you know the name of the font you want to use, rather than clicking the down arrow and locating the font from a long list of fonts try this tip. In the font field on the **Home** tab, highlight the name of the font that's already there and start typing in the name of the font you want to use, Excel will recognise and autofill as you type and change the font in your selection to match.

Change font size

1 Select the cells you want to change.

2 On the **Home** tab, in the 'Font' group, click the current font size **drop-down arrow**.

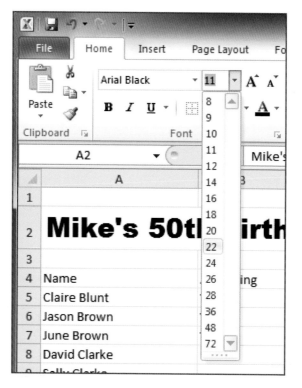

3 On the drop-down menu, move your cursor over a font size to see a live preview on your worksheet.

4 Click a font size to apply it to the selected cells.

To quickly change font size, highlight the number in the font size field and type in the new font size you want to use.

Use the Bold, Italic and Underline commands

1 Select the cells you want to change.

2 On the **Home** tab, in the 'Font' group, click **Bold** (B), **Italic** (I), or **Underline** (U).

Change font colour

1 Select the cells you wish to change.

2 On the **Home** tab, in the 'Font' group, click the 'Font colour' **drop-down arrow**.

3 On the drop-down menu, move your cursor over a colour to see a live preview.

4 Click a font colour to apply it to the selected cells.

Add a border to a cell or cells

1 Select the cell or cells you want to add a border to.

2 On the **Home** tab, in the 'Font' group, click the 'Borders' **drop-down arrow**.

3 From the drop-down menu, select a border style to apply to the selected cells.

Tip

To remove borders, select the cell or cells that have borders and then click the **No Border** option in the 'Borders' button's drop-down menu.

Tip

Click **More Borders** from the Border's drop-down list to access more options for applying borders to cells.

Add a background fill colour

1 Select the cell or cells you want to add a fill colour to.

2 On the **Home** tab, in the 'Font' group, click the 'Fill Color' **drop-down arrow**.

3 On the drop-down menu, move your cursor over a colour to see a live preview.

4 Click a fill colour to apply it to the selected cells.

Change horizontal text alignment

1 Select the cell or cells you want to change.

2 On the **Home** tab, in the 'Alignment' group, select one of the following horizontal alignment options:

- **Align Text Left:** aligns text to the left of a cell.
- **Center:** centres text within a cell.
- **Align Text Right:** aligns text to the right of a cell.

Change vertical text alignment

By default, Excel aligns content to the bottom of a cell, but you can change the vertical alignment to suit your needs.

1 Select the cell or cells you want to change.

2 On the **Home** tab, in the 'Alignment' group, select one of the following vertical alignment options:
- **Top Align:** aligns text to the top of the cell.
- **Middle Align:** centres text vertically.
- **Bottom Align:** aligns text to the bottom of the cell.

File	Home	Insert	Page Layout	Formulas	Data	Review	View

Arial Black 16 Wrap Text

Paste B I U A Merge & Center

Clipboard Font Alignment

A2 fx Mike's 50th

Middle Align

Align text so that it is centered between the top and bottom of the cell.

	A	B		
1				
2	**Mike's 50th birthday party**			
3				
4	**First Name**	**Surname**	**Attending**	**Dietary**
5	David	Clarke	Yes	Chicken
6	Clive	Davis	Yes	Chicken
7	Catherine	Evans	Yes	Chicken
8	Sandra	Evans	Yes	Chicken
9	Hugh	Evans	Yes	Chicken
10	Joseph	Farelly	Yes	Chicken
11	Anna	Thompson	Yes	Chicken
12	Pete	Thompson	Yes	Chicken
13	Sam	Thompson	Yes	Chicken
14	Andy	Graves	Yes	Chicken
15	June	Brown	Yes	Fish
16	Nina	Eastwood	Yes	Fish
17	Andrew	Muller	Yes	Fish
18	Linda	Mumford	Yes	Fish
19	Bridget	Farelly	Yes	Fish
20	Jonathan	Bertrand	Yes	Fish
21	Carmel	Bertrand	Yes	Fish

Format numbers and dates

Along with adjusting font size and colour, Excel lets you choose how numbers in a cell are displayed as a value. For example, you may have created a worksheet to manage your household budget and therefore need to add a £ sign to some of the figures (see the example below). Or you may wish to display your dates in a certain way such as 08/08/2013 rather than 8 August 2013.

Format numbers and dates

1 Select the cells you want to format.

2 On the **Home** tab, in the 'Numbers' group, click the 'Number Format' **drop-down arrow** (this will say 'General' by default).

3 Select the number format you want. You can choose from:

- **General:** this is the default setting. When you enter a value into a cell, Excel looks at the type of number and chooses an appropriate format.
- **Number:** formats a number with decimal places, for example, if you enter 3 in a cell, it will be shown as '3.00'.
- **Currency:** formats a number as currency with a currency symbol, for example, '3' will be shown as '£3.00'.
- **Accounting:** applies a monetary value to a number but aligns currency symbols and decimal places within columns making it easier to work with lots of monetary figures.
- **Short Date:** formats a number as M/D/YYYY, for example 9th October 2013 would be shown as 9/10/2013.
- **Long Date:** formats a number as Weekday, Month DD, YYYY so 9th October 2013 would be shown as Monday, October 09, 2013.
- **Time:** formats a number as HH/MM/SS and adds AM or PM, for example 9:30:00AM.
- **Percentage:** formats a number with decimal places and the percentage symbol, for example '25' will be shown as '25.00%'.
- **Fraction:** formats numbers as fractions using a forward slash, for example '1/4'.

General
No specific format

Number
40.99

Currency
£40.99

Accounting
£40.99

Short Date
09/02/1900

Long Date
09 February 1900

Time
23:45:36

Percentage
4099.00%

Fraction
41

Scientific
4.10E+01

More Number Formats...

- **Scientific:** formats a number in scientific notation.
- **Text:** formats a number as text so a number will be shown as you wrote it. If a cell contains both text and numbers it will be default to this setting.
- **More Number Formats...:** click on this to open the 'Format Cells' dialog box. Here you can customise a format, such as change currency symbols or the number of decimal places shown.

Format Cells

| Number | Alignment | Font | Border | Fill | Protection |

Category:

General
Number
Currency
Accounting
Date
Time
Percentage
Fraction
Scientific
Text
Special
Custom

Sample

£40.99

Decimal places: 2

Symbol: £

Negative
DZD Tamazight (Latin, Algeria)
ETB Amharic
ƒ Papiamentu
fr. French (Switzerland)
Fr. German (Switzerland)
fr. Italian (Switzerland)

-£1,234.
£1,234.
-£1,234.
-£1,234.

Currency formats are used for general monetary values. Use Accounting formats to align decimal points in a column.

OK   Cancel

4 Your number will be formatted according to the option you've chosen.

Tip

There are a couple of ways to change the number formatting for dates from the default US style of showing the month before the day to the UK style, which displays the day first and then the month, so for example, 14/02/2012 rather than 02/14/2012. The best way is to ensure the region settings in Windows 7 itself are set to UK English as this will automatically change how dates are displayed in Excel. Alternatively, you can change it within Excel for selected cells by opening the 'Format Cells' dialog box (on the **Home** tab, click **Format** and then **Format Cells**), then select **English (U.K.)** from the 'Locale (Location)' drop-down list, and click **OK**.

Add a monetary value to a number

1 Select the cell or cells you wish to change.

2 On the **Home** tab, in the 'Number' group, click the 'Number Format' **drop-down arrow**.

3 From the drop-down menu, click **Currency**.

	A	B	C	D	E	F	G	H	I	J	K	L	M
1	Monthly Household budget												
2		Jan	Feb	March	April	May	June	July	Aug	Sep	Oct	Nov	Dec
3	**HOUSE**												
4	Mortgage	£920.00	£920.00	£920.00	£920.00	£920.00	£920.00	£920.00	£920.00	£920.00	£920.00	£920.00	£920.00
5	Gas	£38.00	£38.00	£38.00	£38.00	£38.00	£38.00	£38.00	£38.00	£38.00	£38.00	£38.00	£38.00
6	Electricity	£58.00	£58.00	£58.00	£58.00	£58.00	£58.00	£58.00	£58.00	£58.00	£58.00	£58.00	£58.00
7	Water	£40.00	£40.00	£40.00	£40.00	£40.00	£40.00	£40.00	£40.00	£40.00	£40.00	£40.00	£40.00
8	Council Tax	£150.00	£150.00	£150.00	£150.00	£150.00	£150.00	£150.00	£150.00	£150.00	£150.00	£150.00	£150.00
9	TV licence	£11.60	£11.60	£11.60	£11.60	£11.60	£11.60	£11.60	£11.60	£11.60	£11.60	£11.60	£11.60
10	BT phone	£40.00	£40.00	£40.00	£40.00	£40.00	£40.00	£40.00	£40.00	£40.00	£40.00	£40.00	£40.00
11	Home Insurance	£25.00	£25.00	£25.00	£25.00	£25.00	£25.00	£25.00	£25.00	£25.00	£25.00	£25.00	£25.00
12	House totals	£1,282.60	£1,282.60	£1,282.60	£1,282.60	£1,282.60	£1,282.60	£1,282.60	£1,282.60	£1,282.60	£1,282.60	£1,282.60	£1,282.60
14	**TRANSPORT**												
15	Petrol	110	125	100	132	140	103	78	145	95	120	80	90
16	Car Insurance	30	30	30	30	30	30	30	30	30	30	30	30
17	Road Tax	25	25	25	25	25	25	25	25	25	25	25	25
18	Parking	32	48	24	10	18	24	22	26	34	10	28	30
19	Public transport	45	30	35	60	48	56	34	32	48	42	25	40
20	Transport totals	242	258	214	257	261	238	189	258	232	227	188	215
22	**LIVING**												

4 Click **OK**.

5 For more options or to customise a format (such as change the currency symbol from £ to $), click **More Number Formats...** at the bottom of this menu.

Use **Currency** on the 'Number Format' command for general money figures, and to align decimal points in a column, select **Accounting**.

Conditional formatting rules

Conditional formatting lets you create rules for how and when cells are formatted. You can control the cell font and style, fill colour and border setting, based on the selected cell's content or value. This can help you quickly pick out key data from a busy worksheet with hundreds of rows of information. For example, you may set a conditional formatting rule that turns a cell's fill colour red if the cell's value is greater than 100.

Create a conditional formatting rule

1 Select the cells that you want to add a rule to.

2 On the **Home** tab, in the 'Styles' group, click **Conditional Formatting**.

3 From the drop-down menu select **Highlight Cells Rules** or **Top/Bottom Rules**. Here, 'Highlight Cells Rules' is used.

4 On the resulting menu, select a rule. In this case, **Greater Than....**

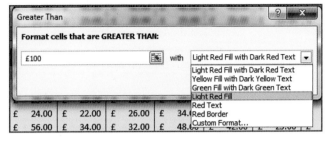

5 In the dialog box, enter a **value**, if applicable. In this example, cells are formatted whose value is greater than £100. You can enter a **cell reference** instead of a number.

6 Select a formatting style from the drop-down menu; in this case, **Light Red Fill**.

7 The formatting is now applied to the selected cells.

Use Excel's preset conditional formatting

Excel has a number of preset rules that let you quickly apply conditional formatting to your cells. They are grouped into three categories:

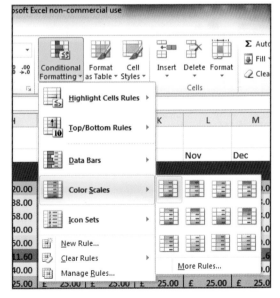

- **Data Bars:** applies a horizontal bar to each cell. The length of the data bar indicates the value in the column. Higher values have longer data bars, and lower values have shorter data bars.
- **Color Scales:** changes the colour of each cell based on its value. Each colour scale uses a two- or three-colour gradient to show the difference in values. For example, in the 'Green – Yellow – Red' colour scale, the highest values are green, average values are yellow, and the lowest values are red.

■ **Icon Sets:** adds an icon to each cell based on its value. In this example using arrows, the direction of the arrow relates to the value of the cell with the highest values showing an arrow directed upwards.

Apply a preset rule

1 Select the cells you want to add the rule to.

2 On the **Home** tab, in the 'Styles' group, click **Conditional Formatting**.

3 From the drop-down menu, select **Data Bars**, **Color Scales** or **Icon Sets**. Then select the desired preset.

4 The conditional formatting is now applied to the selected cells.

Work with themes

A theme is a combination of formats that include colours, fonts and effects. It can be applied to your workbooks to ensure they share a consistent, professional look. Once you select a theme, Excel makes all the design changes with text, charts, graphics, tables and objects altered to reflect the theme you've selected. Excel comes with several built-in themes or you can create your own.

Apply a theme

1 On the **Page Layout** tab, in the 'Themes' group, click **Themes**.

2 Move your cursor over a theme to see a live preview of it.

3 Click on a theme to apply it.

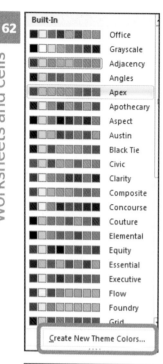

Modify a theme

You may find a theme whose fonts and effects you like, but you'd prefer to use different colours. Excel lets you tweak a theme's colours, fonts and effects for the workbook you're working on. To apply these changes to a new workbook, you can save them as a custom theme.

Change a theme's colours

1 To change the theme colours, on the **Page Layout** tab, in the 'Themes' group, click **Colors**.

2 On the drop-down menu, move your cursor over the colour sets to see a live preview.

3 Click a set of **Theme Colors**, or select **Create New Theme Colors...** to adjust each colour separately.

4 If you have created your own set of theme colours, type a name for the new theme colours in the 'Name' box, and then click **Save**.

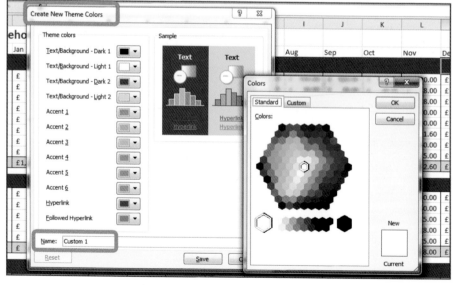

Change a theme's fonts

1 To change the theme fonts, on the **Page Layout** tab, in the 'Themes' group, click **Fonts**.

2 On the drop-down menu, move your cursor over the font sets to see a live preview.

3 Click a set of **Theme Fonts**, or select **Create New Theme Fonts...** to choose each font separately.

4 If you have created your own set of theme fonts, In the 'Name' box, type a name for the new theme fonts, and then click **Save**.

Drop-down menu showing font sets:

- **Black Tie** — Garamond / Garamond
- **Civic** — Georgia / Georgia
- **Clarity** — Arial / Arial
- **Composite** — Calibri / Calibri
- **Concourse** — Lucida Sans Uni... / Lucida Sans Unicode
- **Couture** — Garamond / Garamond
- **Elemental** — Palatino Linotype / Palatino Linotype
- **Equity**
- Create New Theme Fonts...

Create New Theme Fonts

Heading font: Cambria

Body font: Calibri

Sample:

Heading
Body text body text body text.
Body text body text.

Name: Custom 1

Save   Cancel

Change a theme's effects

1 To change the theme effects, on the **Page Layout** tab, in the 'Themes' group, click **Effects**.

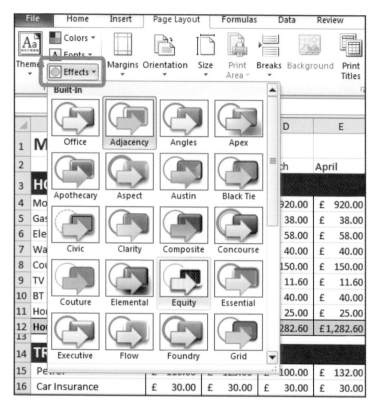

2 On the drop-down menu, move your cursor over the effects sets to see a live preview.

3 Click a set of **Theme Effects**.

Save a theme

1 On the **Page Layout** tab, in the 'Themes' group, click **Themes**.

2 Click **Save Current Theme**.

3 In the **File Name** box, type a name for the theme, and then click **Save**.

Formulas and functions

By reading this chapter you'll get to grips with:

- Creating simple and more complex formulas
- Using functions for easier calculations
- Naming cell ranges

Create formulas

Excel isn't just for storing and displaying your information. Like a calculator, it can perform calculations on numerical data that add, subtract, multiply and divide. So, for example, when working on a household budget, if you want to find out how much money you have left over each month, Excel can help.

Excel performs these calculations using formulas. A formula is a mathematical equation that is used to perform a calculation, for example x+x=z is used to represent the calculation 2+2=4. An Excel formula always starts with an equal sign (=). This is because the cell contains, or is equal to, the formula and its value.

Excel uses standard mathematical operators in its equation. The most-used ones are:

- **A plus sign** for addition (+)
- **A minus sign** for subtraction (-)
- **An asterisk** for multiplication (*)
- **A forward slash** for division (/)

Create a simple formula

1 Select the cell where the answer will appear (B6, for example).

2 Type the equal sign (=).

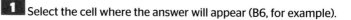

3 Type in the values and the mathematical operator that you want Excel to calculate. For example, '450/40'.

4 Press **Enter**. Excel will perform the calculation and the value will be displayed in the cell you selected.

Create a simple formula using cell references

Excel uses cell references to identify data included in the calculation. So a typical formula using cell references might be '=D6+F4'.

Creating a formula with cell references is usually easier because you can subsequently change the data in your worksheet and it will recalculate automatically without the need to rewrite the values in the formula.

1 Click the cell where you want the answer to appear. In this case, it is B3.

2 Type the equal sign (=).

3 Type the cell address that contains the first number in the equation. In this case, B1.

4 Type the operator required for the formula. In this case, the addition sign (+).

5 Type the cell address that contains the second number in the equation. In this case, it's B2.

	A	B	C	D	E
1	January expenditure	£342.00			
2	February expenditure	£284.00			
3	**TOTAL**	£626.00			
4					
5					

6 Press **Enter**. The formula will be calculated and the value displayed in the cell.

Edit a formula

1 Click on the cell you want to edit.

2 Click on the formula bar and edit the formula. Alternatively, double click the cell to edit the formula directly in the cell.

3 When finished, press **Enter**.

4 The new value will be displayed in the cell.

Create a complex formula

A complex formula has more than one mathematical operation, for example, w+x−y = z. Excel calculates formulas based on the following standard order of operations:

- Parentheses.
- Exponents (to the power of).
- Multiplication and division, whichever comes first.
- Addition and subtraction, whichever comes first.

So the calculation 2+4−3 will be rewritten by Excel as =(2+4)−3 or, more commonly, using cell references such as =(D6+F4)−G8.

As an example, follow these steps for creating a formula using cell references to work out the amount of VAT payable on the items for sale in a club shop: 20%.

1 Click the cell where you want the formula result to appear. In this case, the cell is D3. Type the equal sign (=) and then type an open parenthesis. Click on the cell that contains the first value you want in the formula (in this example, C3).

	A	B	C	D	E
1	Herts Lawn Bowls Club Shop				
2		ITEM NUMBER	PRICE	VAT	QUANTITY
3	Gents White Bowling Trousers	AWT123	£30.99	=(C3/100)*20	2
4	Gents Grey Bowling Trousers	AGT234	£28.99		1

SUM =(C3/100)*20

2 Type the first mathematical operator (for example, the division sign) and value in the formula - in this case, 100 - and then type a closed parenthesis. Type the next mathematical operator (for example, the multiplication sign).

3 Type the next value in the formula, then click **Enter** to calculate your formula.

Work with cell references in formulas

When using formulas, it's important to understand how cell references work. Excel uses three types of cell references in its formulas: relative, absolute and mixed. You need to use the correct one to get accurate results when you copy formulas to another location in the worksheet.

Relative references

By default, Excel uses relative referencing, which means if you want to use the same formula somewhere else in the worksheet, the cell reference will automatically change. For example, if you copy the formula (=A1+B1) into row 3, the formula will change to become (=A3+B3).

Absolute references

In a formula, an absolute cell reference always refers to a cell in a specific location. If the location of the cell that has the formula changes, the absolute reference stays the same. For example, if you copy an absolute reference in cell B2 to cell B3, it stays the same in both cells: =$A$1.

An absolute reference in a formula is shown by the addition of a dollar sign ($) – either before the column reference, row reference, or both.

Mixed references

You can also use a mixed reference in which the column is absolute and the row is relative or vice versa. If you copy a formula, the relative reference automatically adjusts, but the absolute reference stays the same. When creating a mixed reference, use the dollar sign in front of either the column letter or row number that you want to use as the absolute reference. For example, if you copy a mixed reference from cell A2 to B3, it adjusts from =A$1 to =B$1.

Tip

Excel uses relative referencing by default. So when a formula is copied to another cell, the cell references in the formula change to reflect the new location. If you want to use an absolute reference instead remember to insert the $ symbol into the formula.

Create and copy a formula using relative references

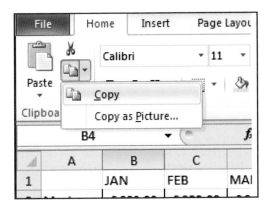

1 Select the cell where you want to enter the formula (for example, B5).

2 Enter the formula to calculate the value you want (for example, add B2+B3+B4).

3 Press **Enter** to calculate the value.

4 Select the cell with the formula you want to copy (in this case, B5) and on the **Home** tab, click **Copy**.

5 Select the cells where you want to paste the formula and on the **Home** tab, click **Paste**.

6 Your formula is copied as a relative reference (C5=C2+C3+C4, D5=D2+D3+D4, and so on) and the values calculated.

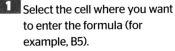

	A	B	C	D	E	F	G	H	I	J	K	L	M	N
1		JAN	FEB	MARCH	APRIL	MAY	JUNE	July	AUG	SEP	OCT	NOV	DEC	
2	Groceries	£250.00	£240.00	£300.00	£278.00	£255.00	£320.00	£298.00	£324.00	£369.00	£270.00	£295.00	£324.00	
3	Child care	£30.00	£30.00	£30.00	£30.00	£30.00	£30.00	£30.00	£30.00	£30.00	£30.00	£30.00	£30.00	
4	Dining out	£25.00	£25.00	£25.00	£25.00	£25.00	£25.00	£25.00	£25.00	£25.00	£25.00	£25.00	£25.00	
5	TOTAL	£305.00	£295.00	£355.00	£333.00	£310.00	£375.00	£353.00	£379.00	£424.00	£325.00	£350.00	£379.00	
6														
7														

C5   fx =C2+C3+C4

Average: £352.55   Count: 11   Sum: £3,878.00   100%

Formulas and functions

Create and copy a formula using an absolute reference

 Select the cell where you want to enter the formula (for example, C4).

 Click on the cell with the first value you want in the formula (for example, B4).

	A	B	C	D	E
	IF	fx	=B4*$B$1		
1	VAT at 20%	0.2			
2					
3	ITEM	Price	VAT		
4	Gents White Bowling Trousers	£ 40.99	=B4*$B$1		
5	Gents Grey Bowling Trousers	£ 48.99			
6	Ladies Blazer	£ 40.99			

3 Type the first mathematical operator. In this example, the multiplication sign.

4 Type the **dollar sign** ($) and the **column letter** of the cell you want as an absolute reference (for example, B).

5 Type the **dollar sign** ($) and the **row number** of the same cell you're making an absolute reference to (for example, 1).

	A	B	C	D	E	F
	IF	fx	=B4*$B$1			
1	VAT at 20%	0.2				
2						
3	ITEM	Price	VAT			
4	Gents White Bowling Trousers	£ 40.99	=B4*$B$1			

6 Press **Enter** to calculate the value.

7 Select the cell you want to copy (for example, C4) and on the **Home** tab, click **Copy**.

8 Select the cells where you want to paste the formula and on the **Home** tab, click **Paste**.

9 The formula is copied using the absolute reference (C5=B5*$B$1, C6=B6*$B$1, and so on) and the values calculated.

Create basic functions

Writing formulas can be tedious and tricky so, if possible, consider using a function. A function is a predefined formula that performs a calculation using specific values in a certain order. Excel comes with hundreds of different, ready-to-use functions, which can save you time and effort.

Excel's functions can be accessed on the 'Formulas' tab in the 'Function Library'. Here you can search for functions based on categories, such as 'Financial', 'Text', 'Date & Time' and more.

Parts of a function

Inserting a function into a formula has to be done in a certain way in order for the function to work correctly. This is how it works using **=SUM(B2:B6)** as an example:

First you must insert an **equal sign** (=), then a **function name** (in this example **SUM**, which will add up the numbers in a range of cells), and then an 'argument' – the information you want the formula to calculate, such as a range of cell references as shown here by **B2:B6**.

Arguments must be enclosed in parentheses (brackets), with individual values or cell references inside the parentheses separated by either colons or commas:

- **Colons** create a reference to a range of cells so, for example, **=AVG(D2:D15)** calculates the average of the cells from D2 through to D15.
- **Commas** separate individual values, cell references and cell ranges in the parentheses. If you use more than one argument, you must separate each with a comma. For example, **=COUNT(B2:B10,B12:B22,B26)** will count all the cell values in the three cell ranges.

Create a basic function

1 Select the cell where you want the answer to appear (D4, for example).

2 Type the **equal sign** (=) and enter the **function name**.

3 Enter the cells for the argument inside the parenthesis.

4 Press **Enter**. The result will appear in the cell you selected.

Use AutoSum to select common functions

Common functions such as SUM (adds all the numbers in a range of cells) and AVG (calculates the average of the values of cells) can be found on the **Home** tab or the **Formulas** tab under the **AutoSum** button.

1 Select the cell where you want the answer to appear (in this example, F15).

2 On the **Formulas** tab, in the 'Functions Library' group, click the 'AutoSum' **drop-down arrow** and then select a function from the menu (in this example, Sum).

3 Select the cells to use in your argument – in this example, a range of cells in column F to total the values.

IF ... =SUM(F3:F14)

Herts Lawn Bowls Club Shop

Herts store	ITEM NUMBER	PRICE	VAT	TOTAL	SURCHARGE
Gents White Bowling Trousers	AWT123	£40.99	£8.20	£49.19	£0.00
Gents Grey Bowling Trousers	AGT234	£48.99	£9.80	£58.79	£0.00
Ladies Blazer	BLZ765	£40.99	£8.20	£49.19	£0.00
Gents Blazer	BLZ236	£40.99	£8.20	£49.19	£0.00
Ladies White Bowling Trousers	LWT987	£30.99	£6.20	£37.19	£5.00
Ladies Grey Bowling Trousers	LGT765	£28.99	£5.80	£34.79	£5.00
Unisex V-neck pullover	UVP675	£21.99	£4.40	£26.39	£5.00
Unisex Waterproof Jacket	UWJ239	£49.99	£10.00	£59.99	£0.00
Ladies Short Sleeve Blouse	SSB779	£12.99	£2.60	£15.59	£5.00
Ladies Waistcoat	LWT569	£17.99	£3.60	£21.59	£5.00
Unisex Polo Shirt	UPS453	£9.99	£2.00	£11.99	£5.00
Bowls bag	BB3498	£59.99	£12.00	£71.99	£0.00
TOTAL				£485.86	=SUM(F3:F14)

4 Press **Enter** and the result appears in the cell you selected.

F18 ... =IF(E16<50,5,0)

Herts Lawn Bowls Club Shop

Herts store	ITEM NUMBER	PRICE	VAT	TOTAL	SURCHARGE
Gents White Bowling Trousers	AWT123	£40.99	£8.20	£49.19	£0.00
Gents Grey Bowling Trousers	AGT234	£48.99	£9.80	£58.79	£0.00
Ladies Blazer	BLZ765	£40.99	£8.20	£49.19	£0.00
Gents Blazer	BLZ236	£40.99	£8.20	£49.19	£0.00
Ladies White Bowling Trousers	LWT987	£30.99	£6.20	£37.19	£5.00
Ladies Grey Bowling Trousers	LGT765	£28.99	£5.80	£34.79	£5.00
Unisex V-neck pullover	UVP675	£21.99	£4.40	£26.39	£5.00
Unisex Waterproof Jacket	UWJ239	£49.99	£10.00	£59.99	£0.00
Ladies Short Sleeve Blouse	SSB779	£12.99	£2.60	£15.59	£5.00
Ladies Waistcoat	LWT569	£17.99	£3.60	£21.59	£5.00
Unisex Polo Shirt	UPS453	£9.99	£2.00	£11.99	£5.00
Bowls bag	BB3498	£59.99	£12.00	£71.99	£0.00
TOTAL				£485.86	£30.00

Do more with functions

Excel has hundreds of functions that you can use with your data. You can find these listed in categories in the Functions Library. Click the **Formulas** tab to access the 'Functions Library'. In the library you'll see the following options:

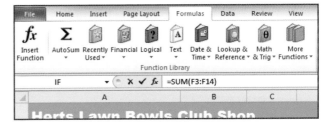

- **Insert Function:** click on this to search for a function. You can enter a description to find exactly what you're looking for.
- **AutoSum:** gives you quick results from common functions.
- **Recently Used:** gives quick access to the functions you've recently used.
- **Financial:** click here for financial functions, such as interest rate for a loan (RATE).
- **Logical:** click here for functions that check the arguments for a condition or value, such as IF, which applies to cells that meet a certain condition, such as containing a value of £100 or more.
- **Text:** click here for functions that work with text in arguments, such as LOWER, which changes text to lowercase.
- **Date & Time:** click here for functions that work with dates and time, such as NOW, which shows the current date.
- **Lookup & Reference:** click here for functions that give results for finding references, such as adding a hyperlink to a cell.
- **Math & Trig:** click here for functions for mathematical arguments, such as rounding values (ROUND).
- **More Functions:** click here for further categories of functions: Statistical, Engineering, Cube, Information and Compatibility.

Add a function from the Function Library

In this example, the 'IF' function is used to add a £5 surcharge to each order that's below a minimum order of £45.

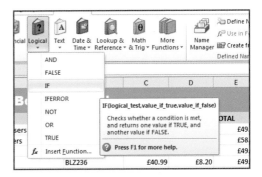

1 Select the cell where you want the answer to appear (in this example, F3).

2 On the **Formulas** tab, in the 'Function Library' group, click a function category. In this example, 'Logical'.

3 Click a **function** from the drop-down menu. In this example, 'IF', which checks if a 'condition' is true and then returns one value if true and another value if false.

4 The 'Function Arguments' dialog box appears with fields that vary depending on the function you've selected. Here, in the 'Logical_test' field, enter the cell(s) you want to use. In this example, 'E3' is entered for the 'IF' function to check the value of this cell.

5 Then directly after the cell reference, type the less than symbol (<) and then the value – in this example it's '45'.

6 Type a value in the 'Value_if_true' fields. In this example, '5' is inserted here as £5 is the amount of money that will be added as a surcharge should the value of E3 be less than 45.

7 Type a value in the 'Value_if_false' field. In this example, '0' is inserted as there is no surcharge for items costing more than £45.

8 Click **OK** and the result will appear in the cell you selected. In this example, the result returned is £0.00 as the order value was more than £45.

	A	B	C	D	E	F	G
1	**Herts Lawn Bowls Club Shop**						
2	**Herts store**	**ITEM NUMBER**	**PRICE**	**VAT**	**TOTAL**	**SURCHARGE**	
3	Gents White Bowling Trousers	AWT123	£40.99	£8.20	£49.19	£0.00	
4	Gents Grey Bowling Trousers	AGT234	£48.99	£9.80	£58.79	£0.00	
5	Ladies Blazer	BLZ765	£40.99	£8.20	£49.19	£0.00	
6	Gents Blazer	BLZ236	£40.99	£8.20	£49.19	£0.00	
7	Ladies White Bowling Trousers	LWT987	£30.99	£6.20	£37.19	£5.00	
8	Ladies Grey Bowling Trousers	LGT765	£28.99	£5.80	£34.79	£5.00	
9	Unisex V-neck pullover	UVP675	£21.99	£4.40	£26.39	£5.00	
10	Unisex Waterproof Jacket	UWJ239	£49.99	£10.00	£59.99	£0.00	
11	Ladies Short Sleeve Blouse	SSB779	£12.99	£2.60	£15.59	£5.00	
12	Ladies Waistcoat	LWT569	£17.99	£3.60	£21.59	£5.00	
13	Unisex Polo Shirt	UPS453	£9.99	£2.00	£11.99	£5.00	
14	Bowls bag	BB3498	£59.99	£12.00	£71.99	£0.00	
15	TOTAL				£485.86		
16							

F3 · fx =IF(E3<45,5,0)

9 You can then copy and paste or drag using the fill handles (see pages 40-1) to apply the formula to a range of cells.

Use Insert Function

The 'Insert Function' dialog box makes it easy to find the right function for what you want to do. It also provides information about the arguments that the function uses.

1 Select the cell where you want the answer to your function to appear.

2 On the **Formulas** tab, in the 'Function Library', click **Insert Function**.

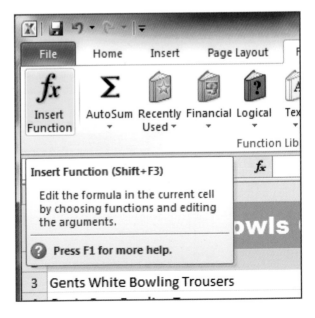

Formulas and functions

Insert Function

Search for a function:

count cells with text

Go

Or select a category: Most Recently Used ▾

Select a function:

COUNTA
COUNT
AVERAGE
IF
SUM
HYPERLINK
MAX

COUNTA(value1,value2,...)
Counts the number of cells in a range that are not empty.

Help on this function   OK   Cancel

3 In the 'Insert Function' dialog box, type a brief description of the function you're searching for and click **Go**.

4 Select a function in the 'Select a function' list box. A description of the selected function can be seen at the bottom of the dialog box.

5 Click **OK**.

Function Arguments

COUNTA

Value1 A3:A14   = {"Gents White Bowling Trousers";"Ge...
Value2 A18:A29   = {"Gents White Bowling Trousers";"Ge...
Value3   = number

= 24

Counts the number of cells in a range that are not empty.

Value2: value1,value2,... are 1 to 255 arguments representing the values and cells you want to count. Values can be any type of information.

Formula result = 24

Help on this function   OK   Cancel

6 The 'Function Arguments' dialog box will appear. Here you enter the arguments for the function. Insert the cursor in the first field (Value1) and then enter or select the cell(s) you want to use (in this example, cells A3:A14).

7 Insert the cursor in the next field (Value2) and then enter or select the cell(s) you wish to use (in this example, cells A18–A29).

8 Click **OK** and the result will appear in the cell you selected in Step 1.

Work with What-If Analysis

A useful feature of Excel are the What-If Analysis tools, which let you see the input values required to achieve a specific goal, without having to edit formulas. For example, you can use the Goal Seek tool to work out what size mortgage loan you can afford at a certain interest rate and monthly payment.

Use Goal Seek to see maximum mortgage loan

In this example, the worksheet shows the mortgage loan, term in years, annual interest rate and monthly payment. The monthly payment has previously been calculated using a function called 'PMT' – a financial function used to work out loan repayments.

So in this example, the PMT function has been applied in the 'Monthly payment' cell (D4) using the following parameters – (C4/12,B4*12,A4):

- The annual interest rate typed into C4 and divided (/) by 12 to get the monthly rate of interest.
- The term in years typed into B4 and multiplied (*) by 12 to get the number of months.
- The loan amount typed into A4, expressed as a negative number.

Using the Goal Seek tool it is then possible to change the monthly repayment figure to see what effect this has on the amount of money that can be borrowed.

 Click on the cell that has the formula – in this case **D4**.

 On the **Data** tab, in the 'Data Tools' group, click **What-If Analysis**.

3 From the drop-down menu, click **Goal Seek....**

4 A dialog box will appear containing three fields:
- **Set cell:** this is the cell that contains the desired goal/result (in this case, the monthly payment).
- **To value:** this is the result that is wanted. In this example, it is set to 900, as the maximum monthly payment that can be made is £900.
- **By changing cell:** this is the cell where Goal Seek will place its answer (in this case, the mortgage loan amount in A4).

5 Click **OK**. The dialog box will tell you whether or not 'Goal Seek' was able to find a solution.

Goal Seek Status [?] [X]

Goal Seeking with Cell D4 found a solution.

Step

Pause

Target value: 900
Current value: £900.00

OK   Cancel

6 Click **OK** and the result will appear in the cell you selected.

Book2 - Microsoft Excel non-commercial use

File   Home   Insert   Page Layout   Formulas   Data   Review   View

Connections
Properties
Get External   Refresh   Edit Links
Data ▾   All ▾
Connections

A↓ A Z
Z↓ Z A
Sort   Filter
Sort & Filter

Clear
Reapply
Advanced

Text to   Remove
Columns Duplicates
Data Tools

Data Val
Consolid
What-If

A4   fx   -154107.593169146

	A	B	C	D	E
1	**Mortgage Payment Plan**				
2					
3	Loan Amount	Term	Annual Interest rate	Monthly payment	
4	-£ 154,107.59	25	4.99%	£900.00	
5					
6					
7					
8					

In this example, the solution - the amount that is is possible to borrow by paying £900 per month - is calculated at £154,107.59 and shown in cell A4.

Name cell ranges

To make working with formulas and functions easier, you can give a descriptive name to a cell or range of cells. For example, by first assigning the name 'MonthlyTotal' to a range of cells, you can then use the formula **= SUM(MonthlyTotal)** rather than **= SUM(B2:B12)**.

Name cells

1 Select the cell or cell range that you want to name. To select non-adjacent cells, press the **Ctrl** key as you select each one.

2 On the **Formulas** tab, in the 'Defined Names' group, click **Define Name**.

⌨ Define Name ▾

File	Home	Insert	Page Layout	Formulas	Data	Review	View

fx Insert Function	Σ AutoSum ▾	Recently Used ▾	Financial ▾	Logical ▾	A Text ▾	Date & Time ▾	Lookup & Reference ▾	θ Math & Trig ▾	More Functions ▾	Name Manager	⌨ Define Name ▾ *fx* Use in Formula ⌨ Create from Sel

Function Library | Defined Names

B4	▾	*fx*	920

◢	A	B	C	D	E	F	G	H
1	**Monthly Household budget**							
2		Jan	Feb	March	April	May	June	July
3	**HOUSE**							
4	Mortgage	£ 920.00	£ 920.00	£ 920.00	£ 920.00	£ 920.00	£ 920.00	£ 920.
5	Gas	£ 38.00	£ 38.00	£ 38.00	£ 38.00	£ 38.00	£ 38.00	£ 38.
6	Electricity	£ 58.00	£ 58.00	£ 58.00	£ 58.00	£ 58.00	£ 58.00	£ 58.
7	Water	£ 40.00	£ 40.00	£ 40.00	£ 40.00	£ 40.00	£ 40.00	£ 40.
8	Council Tax	£ 150.00	£ 150.00	£ 150.00	£ 150.00	£ 150.00	£ 150.00	£ 150.

3 In the 'New Name' dialog box, type a name for the range in the 'Name' field. A name can be up to 255 characters long and can contain upper and lower case letters. However, names must follow these conventions:

New Name	? ✕
Name:	Jan01housebills
Scope:	Workbook ▾
Comment:	
Refers to:	='2011'!$B$4:$B$11
	OK Cancel

- The first character must be a letter, an underscore, or a backslash. The other can be letters, numbers, full stops and underscore characters.
- No spaces are allowed.
- Names cannot be the same as a cell address. For example, you can't use B52 or U2.

4 Click **OK**.

Use a named range

1 At the left end of the Formula bar, click the 'Name' box
drop-down arrow.

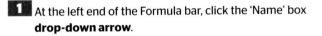

| | File | Home | Insert | Page Layout | Formulas | Data | Review | View |

| Jan01housebills | ▼ | f_x | 920 |

	A	B	C	D	E	F
Feb01housebills						
Jan01housebills		ehold budget				
Jan01transport						
2		Jan	Feb	March	April	May
3	**HOUSE**					
4	Mortgage	£ 920.00	£ 920.00	£ 920.00	£ 920.00	£ 920.
5	Gas	£ 38.00	£ 38.00	£ 38.00	£ 38.00	£ 38.
6	Electricity	£ 58.00	£ 58.00	£ 58.00	£ 58.00	£ 58.
7	Water	£ 40.00	£ 40.00	£ 40.00	£ 40.00	£ 40.
8	Council Tax	£ 150.00	£ 150.00	£ 150.00	£ 150.00	£ 150.
9	TV licence	£ 11.60	£ 11.60	£ 11.60	£ 11.60	£ 11.
10	BT phone	£ 40.00	£ 40.00	£ 40.00	£ 40.00	£ 40.
11	Home Insurance	£ 25.00	£ 25.00	£ 25.00	£ 25.00	£ 25.
12	**House totals**	£1,282.60	£1,282.60	£1,282.60	£1,282.60	£1,282.

2 Select the range name you want to access.

3 Excel highlights the named cells.

**Viewing your images on a
computer screen is no indicator
of print quality. This is because
screens display images at 72ppi
(pixels per inch), but for a good-
quality print you need to print on
photo paper at 300ppi.**

Manage named ranges

If you have lots of named ranges in your workbook, use the Name Manager to track and manage them. For example, you may want to check the value and reference of a name, view or edit descriptive comments, or change the scope (whether it is limited to just this worksheet or to the entire workbook). You can also sort and filter the list of names (see pages 116-29), and easily add or delete names here.

1 On the **Formulas** tab, in the 'Defined Names' group, click **Name Manager**.

2 In the 'Name Manager' dialog box you can see more information about each name including the current reference for the name (what cells it applies to), the current value (such as the results of a formula) and the scope of the name.

3 To see just a subset of the named ranges, click on **Filter** and from the drop-down menu click an option such as **Names Scoped to Workbook**.

Select	To
Names Scoped To Worksheet	Show only the names that are local to a worksheet
Names Scoped To Workbook	Show only the names that applied to the whole workbook
Names With Errors	Show only the names with values that contain errors (such as #VALUE, or #NAME)
Names Without Errors	Show only the names with values that don't have errors
Defined Names	Show only names that you or Excel have defined, such as a print area
Table Names	Display only table names

 Click **Close** to close the 'Name Manager' dialog box.

Photos and graphics

By reading this chapter you'll get to grips with:

- Adding photos and images to your workbooks
- Working with shapes and tables
- Inserting text boxes and WordArt

Add images

You can liven up your spreadsheets by adding a picture or two or a piece of clip art. You can add a picture from a file (such as a photo you've taken), copy one from a web page or use one of Excel's many ClipArt images.

Add clip art

1 Open the workbook that you want to add clip art to.

2 On the **Insert** tab, in the 'Illustrations' group, click **Clip Art**.

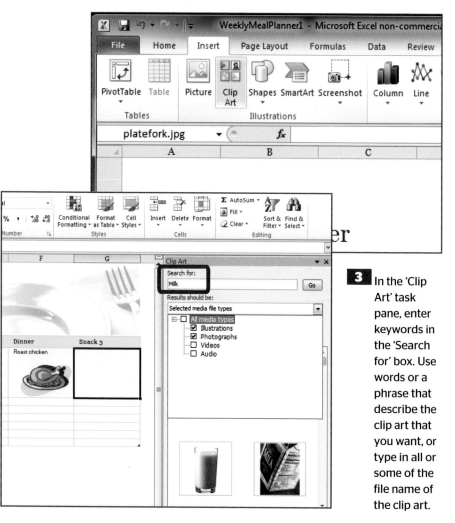

3 In the 'Clip Art' task pane, enter keywords in the 'Search for' box. Use words or a phrase that describe the clip art that you want, or type in all or some of the file name of the clip art.

4 To limit the search results to a specific media type, click the 'Results should be' **drop-down arrow** and deselect the check boxes next to 'Illustrations', 'Photographs', 'Videos' or 'Audio' as required.

5 To expand your search to include clip art on the web, click the **Find more at Office.com** content check box. Otherwise the search will be limited to your computer hard drive.

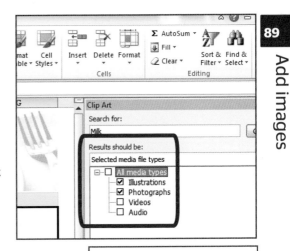

6 Click **Go**.

7 In the list of results, click the clip art to insert it. It will appear in your worksheet.

Jargon buster
Clip art Ready-made artwork that's included with Microsoft Office or can be downloaded from the web.

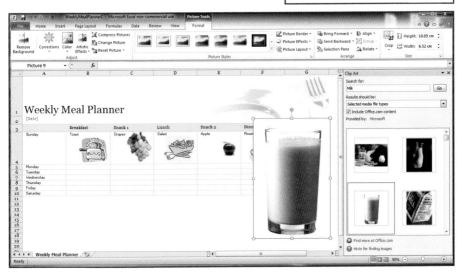

BE CAREFUL!
While it's easy to copy and paste pictures and even video from websites, be sure to check the copyright of these items beforehand. Check the website for copyright notices. Copyright is owned by the person who created the picture or video. It's illegal to copy and use anything protected by copyright, without the permission of the copyright owner.

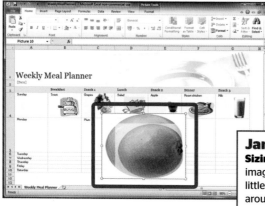

Insert a picture from a file

1 Place your cursor in the worksheet where you wish the image to be.

2 On the **Insert** tab, in the 'Illustrations' group, click **Picture**.

3 The 'Insert Picture' dialog box appears. Choose the picture file you want and click **Insert** to place it in your document.

Insert a picture from a web page

You can drag a picture from a web page into your open workbook. However, avoid dragging a picture that has a link to a web page. If you do, it will appear in your document as a link (a line of text giving the address of the linked web page) rather than the image itself.

Resize clip art or a picture

1 Select the clip art or picture you've placed in the worksheet.

2 Drag a sizing handle away from or towards the centre of the image to resize. To keep the image's proportions, press and hold **Shift** while you drag the sizing handle.

Jargon buster

Sizing handles When you click a shape, image or piece of clip art, a border with little white squares and circles will appear around it. These are the sizing handles. Click and drag on the squares to change the height or width, or on the circles to make the whole object smaller or bigger.

Edit images

Once you have placed images in your worksheet, you can make changes to them using Excel's picture tools. There are lots of ways to adjust your images including changing their colour or brightness, cropping or compressing pictures, and adding all manner of borders and artistic effects.

Crop an image

1 Select the image you want to crop.

2 On the **Format** tab, in the 'Size' group, click **Crop**.

3 Black cropping handles appear around your picture – similar to those used to resize an image. Click and drag a handle to crop an image. Clicking on the corner handles simultaneously crops the image horizontally and vertically.

4 When you've finished, click **Crop** again to apply the crop.

Photos and graphics

Crop an image to a shape

You can use Excel's crop tool to crop to a specific shape.

1 Select the image you want to work with.

2 On the **Format** tab, in the 'Size' group, click on the 'Crop' **drop-down arrow** and select **Crop to Shape**.

3 From the drop-down menu, choose a suitable shape.

4 The image will take the shape you have selected.

Remove an image background

1 Click on the image.

2 On the **Format** tab, in the 'Adjust' group, click **Remove Background**.

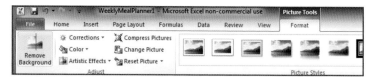

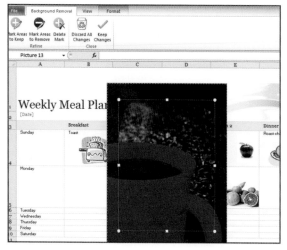

3 Excel guesses which part of the image is the background. It colours this area pink and draws a box with selection handles around the part of the image that will remain.

4 Adjust the selection handles so that all the area you wish to keep is in the box.

5 To change the areas selected as background use the 'Mark Areas to Keep' and 'Mark Areas to Remove' commands:

■ To show which areas of the image you want to keep, click **Mark Areas to Keep**. The cursor changes into a pencil. Click and drag to draw a line in that region of the image.

■ If you want to remove a section of the background that hasn't been automatically selected, click **Mark Areas to Remove**. The cursor changes into a pencil. Click and drag to draw a line in that region of the image.

6 Once you have made your corrections, Excel will then readjust the image.

7 Click **Keep Changes**. All of the pink areas will be removed from the image.

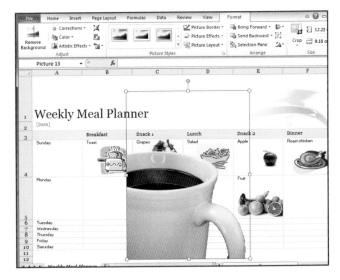

Add a border to an image

1 Select the image.

2 On the **Format** tab, in the 'Picture Styles' group, click **Picture Border**.

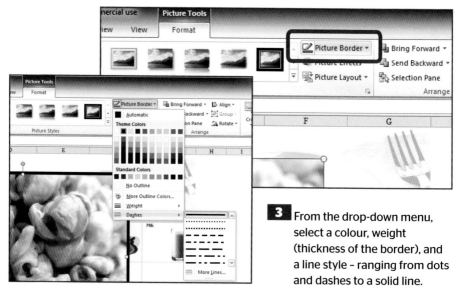

3 From the drop-down menu, select a colour, weight (thickness of the border), and a line style – ranging from dots and dashes to a solid line.

Change image brightness and contrast

1 Select the image.

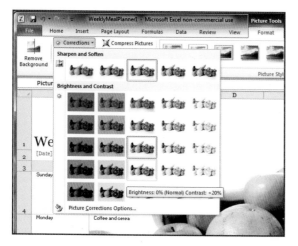

2 On the **Format** tab, in the 'Adjust' group, click **Corrections**. A drop-down menu will appear.

3 To sharpen or soften your picture, move your cursor over the 'Sharpen and Soften' presets to see a live preview of how your image will look with the preset applied. Click on a preset to apply it.

4 To adjust the brightness, move your cursor over the 'Brightness and Contrast' presets to see a live preview of how your image will look with the preset applied.

5 Click on a preset to apply it.

Adjust image colour

1 Select the image.

2 On the **Format** tab, in the 'Adjust' group, click **Color**. A drop-down menu will appear.

3 Here you can choose a preset for each of the following options:
- **Color Saturation:** changes the strength of colours in the image.
- **Color Tone:** affects colour 'temperature' – from cool (more blue) to warm (more red).
- **Recolor:** changes the overall colour of the image. This option can be used to turn an image into black and white or give it a different colour.

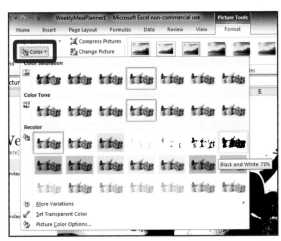

Apply an artistic effect

1 Select the picture.

2 On the **Format** tab, in the 'Adjust' group, click **Artistic Effects**.

3 On the drop-down menu, move your cursor over a preset to see a live preview.

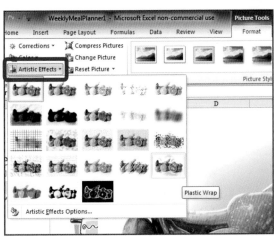

Click on a preset to apply it.

5 You can adjust the settings for an effect, click **Artistic Effects** and then select **Artistic Effect Options...**.

Apply a picture style

1 Select the picture.

2 On the **Format** tab, click the **More drop-down arrow** to show all available picture styles.

3 Move your cursor over a picture style to see a live preview of the style in your document.

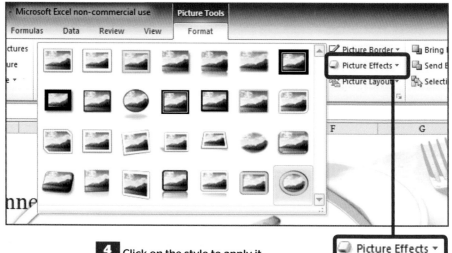

4 Click on the style to apply it.

5 To fine-tune your chosen picture style, click **Picture Effects** to see the 'Effects' drop-down menu.

Tip
You can also format a clip art image or picture using the 'Format Picture' dialog box. Select the picture or clip art and on the **Format** tab click the small arrow at the bottom right corner of the 'Picture Styles' group to launch the dialog box. Once open, select an appropriate tab and makes changes as desired. When finished, click **Close**.

Work with shapes

Add impact to your spreadsheet by incorporating shapes such as arrows, lines, squares, stars, flowchart shapes and banners.

Add a shape

1 With your workbook open, on the **Insert** tab, in the 'Illustrations' group, click **Shapes**.

2 Click on the shape that you want.

3 Click anywhere in your workbook, and then drag to place the shape at the size you want.

4 Release the mouse button.

Move a shape

1 Click on the shape.

2 Hover the cursor over one of the box's edges until it changes into a cross with arrows on each end.

3 Click and drag the shape to the desired location on the page.

Resize a shape

1 Click on the shape to select it.

2 Click and drag one of the sizing handles on the corners and sides of the box until it is the desired size.

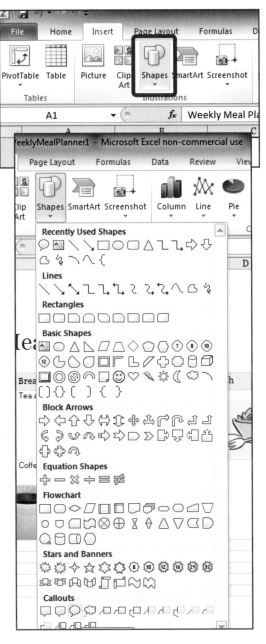

Change shape style

1 Select the shape.

2 On the **Format** tab, in the 'Shape Styles' group, click the **More drop-down arrow** to show more style options.

3 Move your cursor over the styles to see a live preview of the style in your document. Select a style.

Fill with colour

1 Select the shape.

2 On the **Format** tab, in the 'Shape Styles' group, click **Shape Fill**.

3 From the drop-down menu, select either a colour, **No Fill** or **More Fill Colors...** for custom colour. You can also add a picture, gradient or texture to the shape.

4 To adjust the transparency of the shape's fill, click **More Fill Colors...** and in the 'Colors' dialog box, click the **Custom** tab.

5 At the bottom of the dialog box, move the **Transparency** slider, or enter a number in the box next to the slider. You can adjust the percentage of the transparency from 0% (fully opaque, the default setting) to 100% (fully transparent).

Change the shape outline

1 Select the shape.

2 On the **Format** tab, in the 'Shape Styles' group, click **Shape Outline**.

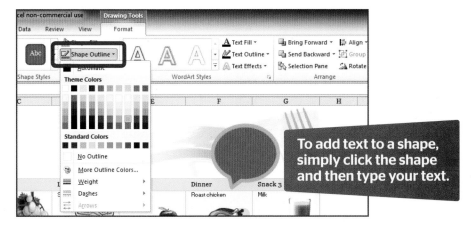

> To add text to a shape, simply click the shape and then type your text.

3 From the drop-down menu, choose an outline colour, weight (thickness), and line style.

Add shadow effects

1 Select the shape.

2 On the **Format** tab, in the 'Shape Styles' group, click **Shape Effects**.

3 From the drop-down menu, move your cursor over 'Shadow' to see a list of shadow presets. Move your cursor over the options to see a live preview of the effect in your document.

4 Click a shadow effect to apply it to your shape.

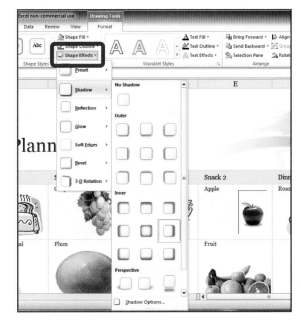

Rotate a shape in 3D

1 Select the shape.

2 On the **Format** tab, in the 'Shape Styles' group, click **Shape Effects**.

3 Move your cursor over '3-D Rotation'. A drop-down menu will appear. Choose a rotation preset.

4 For more precise control, click **3-D Rotation Options...** to type in custom values.

Apply a bevel effect

1 Select the shape.

2 On the **Format** tab, in the 'Shape Styles' group, click **Shape Effects**.

3 Move your cursor over 'Bevel'. A drop-down menu will appear. Choose a bevel preset.

4 You can also click **3-D Options...** at the bottom of the drop-down menu to type in custom values. In addition, you can choose the shape's material to give it a plastic or metal look as well as change the lighting type that determines how a shape is illuminated.

Style text with WordArt

Use the WordArt styling tool to add impact to headings and other text in your workbook. You can specify fill and line colour, add shadows or bevels or create special text effects such as curved, slanted or 3-D text.

Add WordArt

1 On the **Insert** tab, in the 'Text' group, click **WordArt**.

2 Click a WordArt style. A box will appear on the worksheet.

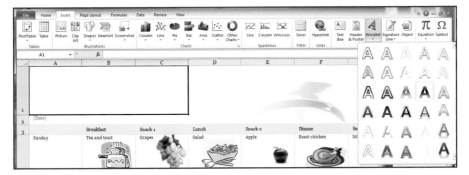

3 Type your text and position the text box where you want it on the worksheet.

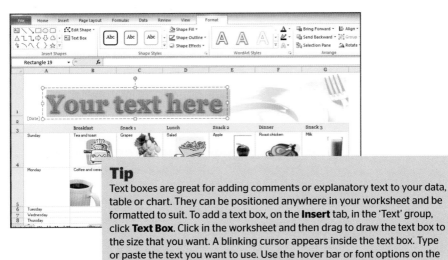

Tip

Text boxes are great for adding comments or explanatory text to your data, table or chart. They can be positioned anywhere in your worksheet and be formatted to suit. To add a text box, on the **Insert** tab, in the 'Text' group, click **Text Box**. Click in the worksheet and then drag to draw the text box to the size that you want. A blinking cursor appears inside the text box. Type or paste the text you want to use. Use the hover bar or font options on the **Home** tab to change the formatting of the text.

Add or modify effects

 1 Select the text box, or some text inside the text box.

 2 On the **Format** tab, in the 'WordArt Styles' group, click on one of the following buttons:

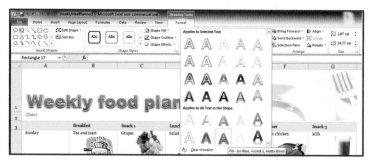

- **WordArt Styles gallery:** to select a new style. Click the **More drop-down arrow** to see additional styles.
- **Text Fill:** modifies the text colour, gradient or pattern.
- **Text Outline:** changes the outer edges of the text.
- **Text Effects:** adds special effects such as shadow, reflection, rotation and bevel.

3 Hover your cursor over a preset to see a live preview.

4 Select a preset and the effect will be applied to your text. You can combine several different WordArt effects on one piece of text.

Rotate or flip objects

You can change how pictures, shapes, WordArt and other objects look by rotating them or flipping them to create a mirror image.

Rotate an object

1 Click the picture, shape, text box or WordArt that you want to rotate.

2 Drag the rotational handle (the green circle) in the direction that you want to rotate the shape.

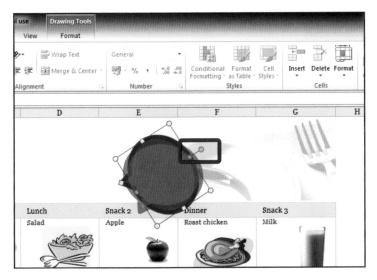

3 Alternatively, you can do the following after you have clicked on the picture, shape, text box or WordArt that you want to rotate:

■ On the **Format** tab, in the 'Arrange' group, click **Rotate**, then click either **Rotate Right 90°** or **Rotate Left 90°**.

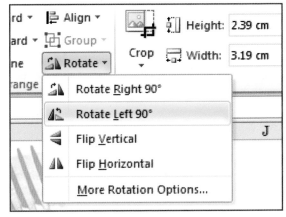

4 To specify an exact rotation click **More Rotation Options...**. Then in the resulting dialog box (this will be called 'Format Picture' or 'Format Shape', depending on what type of object you clicked on in Step 3), click **Size** in the left pane, and in the 'Size' pane, under 'Size and rotate', enter the amount that you want to rotate the object in the 'Rotation' box.

Flip an object

1 Click the picture, shape, text box or WordArt that you want to flip.

2 Do one of the following:
- To flip a picture, under Picture Tools, click the **Format** tab.
- To flip a shape, text box, or WordArt, under Drawing Tools, click the **Format** tab.

3 In the 'Arrange' group, click **Rotate**, and then do one of the following actions:
- To flip the object vertically, click **Flip Vertical**.
- To flip the object horizontally, click **Flip Horizontal**.

Arrange shapes and objects

It can be fiddly and time-consuming positioning objects such as shapes and text boxes individually. Fortunately, Excel has several tools that can help you quickly arrange objects in your worksheet.

Align two or more objects

1 Select the objects to be aligned by holding down the **Ctrl** key and clicking on each in turn.

2 On the **Format** tab, in the 'Arrange' group, click **Align**.

3 From the drop-down menu, select one of the following alignment options:
- **Align Left:** aligns objects left.
- **Align Center:** aligns objects vertically through their centre.
- **Align Right:** aligns objects to the right.
- **Align Top:** aligns objects to their top edges.
- **Align Middle:** aligns two or more objects horizontally through their middles.
- **Align Bottom:** aligns objects to their bottom edges.
- **Distribute Horizontally:** aligns three or more objects so they are equally spaced horizontally.
- **Distribute Vertically:** aligns three or more objects so they are equally spaced vertically.
- **Snap to Grid:** when selected, using any of the align options, aligns the objects to the nearest grid intersection.
- **Snap to Shape:** when selected, aligns objects to gridlines that go through the horizontal and vertical edges of other objects.
- **View Gridlines:** turns gridline display off and on.

4 The objects will align to each other based on which option you choose to select.

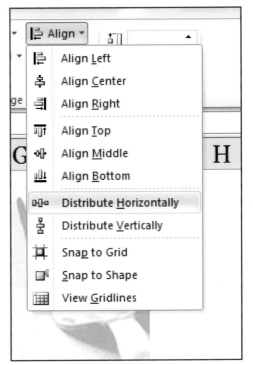

Photos and graphics

Stack objects

You can stack items so that one appears in front of another or even change the order in which each appears on the worksheet.

 Select the object you wish to move.

2 On the **Format** tab, in the 'Arrange' group, choose one of the following options:

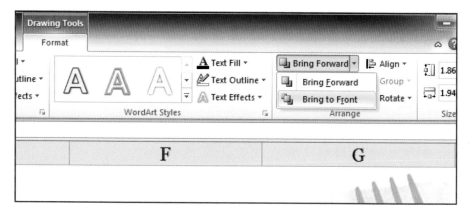

- ■ To move the object one step nearer the front of the stack, click **Bring Forward**.
- ■ To bring it to the top of the stack, click the 'Bring Forward' **drop-down arrow**, and then click **Bring to Front**.
- ■ To move it in front of text, click the 'Bring Forward' **drop-down arrow**, and then click **Bring in Front of Text**.
- ■ To move it one step down in the stack, click **Send Backward**.
- ■ To move it to the bottom of the stack, click the 'Send Backward' **drop-down arrow**, and then click **Send to Back**.
- ■ To move it behind text, click the 'Send Backward' **drop-down arrow,** and then click **Send Behind Text**.

Group objects

Rather than selecting multiple objects each time you want to move or change them, you can group shapes, text boxes and other elements into one object. You can then rotate, flip, move and resize the objects at the same time as if they were a single item. You can also change the format of all the items within a group at once – for example, by adding a fill colour or shape effects.

Group objects

1 Select the objects you wish to group by holding down the **Ctrl** key and clicking on each in turn.

2 On the **Format** tab, in the 'Arrange' group, click the **Group** button, and then click **Group**.

3 The objects will now be grouped. There will be a single box with sizing handles around the entire group to show that they are one object.

Ungroup objects

1 Select the group that you want to ungroup.

2 On the **Format** tab, in the 'Arrange' group, click **Group**, and then click **Ungroup**.

3 The items will appear ungrouped.

Even after you've grouped together a number of objects, you can still select a single object within the group. Select the group, and then click the individual object that you want to select.

Add SmartArt graphics

SmartArt graphics are predrawn diagrams and charts that make it easy to illustrate the data in your Excel workbook. Best of all, you can edit and alter the diagrams without having to fiddle with their shape, size and alignment, as SmartArt graphics automatically adjust to maintain their overall shape and design.

Create a SmartArt graphic

1 Click on the worksheet where you want the SmartArt graphic to be placed.

2 On the **Insert** tab, in the 'Illustration' group, click **SmartArt**.

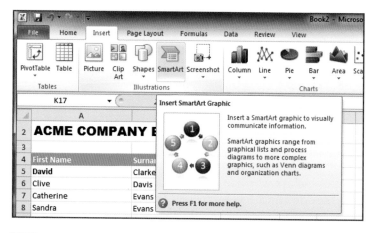

3 On the dialog box that appears, in the left-hand pane, select a category of SmartArt graphics (in this case, **Hierarchy**).

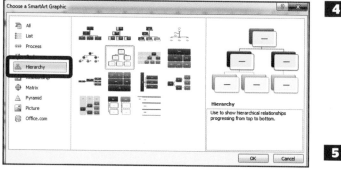

4 In the centre pane, click on one of the layouts in this category to see a more detailed view in the right pane of the dialog box.

5 Click a SmartArt graphic and click **OK**.

Add text to a SmartArt graphic

1 Select the graphic. Click either of the arrows on the left side of the graphic.

2 Enter text next to each bullet in the task pane. It appears in the graphic, resizing automatically to fit inside the shape.

Add or delete a shape to an existing SmartArt graphic

1 Select the SmartArt graphic that you want to add a shape to.

2 From the **Design** tab, in the 'Graphic' group, click **Add Shape**.

3 Click the shape that's positioned closest to where you want to add the new shape.

4 Select **Add Shape After** or **Add Shape Before**.

5 If you want to add a superior or a subordinate shape, select either the **Add Shape Above** or **Add Shape Below** options.

6 To delete a shape within a SmartArt graphic, click the shape, and then press the **Delete** key on your keyboard. To delete the entire SmartArt graphic, click the border of the SmartArt graphic, and then press **Delete**.

Photos and graphics

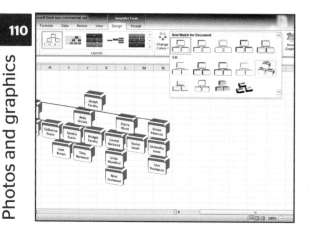

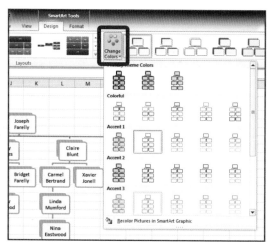

Change the SmartArt style

1 Select the graphic.

2 On the **Design** tab, in the 'SmartArt Styles' group, click the **More drop-down arrow** to view all the styles.

3 Move your cursor over a style to see a live preview.

4 Click a style to apply it.

Change the colour of a SmartArt graphic

There is a wide range of colour schemes to use with SmartArt graphics.

1 Click the SmartArt graphic.

2 On the Design tab, in the 'SmartArt Styles' group, click **Change Colors**.

3 From the drop-down menu, choose a colour scheme.

To change the look of just one shape in a SmartArt graphic, select the shape and click the **Format** tab. You can then change the shape style, colour, effects and other settings.

Tip

To quickly move shapes in a SmartArt graphic up (promote) and down (demote) use the task pane. Place the cursor in the task pane, press **Tab** to demote a shape. Press the **Backspace key** (or **Shift-Tab**) to promote a shape.

View and analyse data

By reading this chapter you'll get to grips with:

- Sorting and filtering data
- Formatting data as tables and pivot tables
- Creating charts and sparkline graphics

Freeze rows and columns

Excel lets you freeze or lock panes so that top rows or left-hand columns remain visible even when you scroll to another area of the spreadsheet. This is really useful when working on a large spreadsheet, as you can see column headers or row labels at all times when scrolling through.

Freeze a row

1 Select the row below the row or rows that you want to keep visible. For example, if you want rows 1 and 2 to always appear at the top of the worksheet as you scroll, select row 3.

2 On the **View** tab, in the 'Window' group, click **Freeze Panes**.

3 From the drop-down menu, click **Freeze Panes**.

4 A solid black line under row 2 shows that the rows are frozen, keeping column labels in place as you scroll downwards.

Freeze a column

1 Select the column to the right of the columns you want to freeze. For example, if you want column A and B to always appear on the left of the worksheet as you scroll, then select column C.

2 On the **View** tab, in the Window group, click **Freeze Panes**.

3 From the drop-down menu, click **Freeze Panes**.

4 A solid black line appears to the right of the frozen area. Scroll across the worksheet to see the columns to the right of the frozen columns.

Freeze both rows and columns

You can freeze both rows and columns at the same time.

1 To lock both rows and columns, click the cell below and to the right of the rows and columns that you want to keep visible when you scroll.

2 Click the **View** tab.

3 In the 'Window' group, click **Freeze Panes**.

4 From the drop-down menu, click **Freeze Panes**.

5 A solid black line appears under and to the right of the frozen area.

Unfreeze panes

1 Click the **View** tab.

2 In the 'Window' group, click **Freeze Panes**.

3 From the drop-down menu click **Unfreeze Panes**. The panes will be unfrozen and the black lines will disappear.

non-commercial use							
Arrange All	Freeze Panes ▾	Split / Hide / Unhide	View Side by Side / Synchronous Scrolling / Reset Window Position	Save Workspace	Switch Windows ▾	Macros ▾ / Macros

Unfreeze Panes
Unlock all rows and columns to scroll through the entire worksheet.

Freeze Top Row
Keep the top row visible while scrolling through the rest of the worksheet.

Freeze First Column
Keep the first column visible while scrolling through the rest of the worksheet.

	L	M
Ju		
	Nov	Dec

).00	£	920.00	£	920.00	£	920.00	£	920.00	£	920.00	£ 920.00
3.00	£	38.00	£	38.00	£	38.00	£	38.00	£	38.00	£ 38.00
3.00	£	58.00	£	58.00	£	58.00	£	58.00	£	58.00	£ 58.00
).00	£	40.00	£	40.00	£	40.00	£	40.00	£	40.00	£ 40.00
).00	£	150.00	£	150.00	£	150.00	£	150.00	£	150.00	£ 150.00
.60	£	11.60	£	11.60	£	11.60	£	11.60	£	11.60	£ 11.60

Split a worksheet into panes

If you need to compare information from different sections of a worksheet, you can split the window either vertically or horizontally into separate panes. You can then scroll to a particular area of the worksheet in one pane while maintaining the view in the other pane.

Split a worksheet horizontally into two panes

1 Click the split box that's above the vertical scroll bar. The cursor will turn into a double-arrow.

2 Holding down the mouse button, drag downwards until you reach the row at which you want to divide the worksheet. You'll see a grey dividing line as you drag that shows where the window will be split.

3 Release the mouse button to divide the window into two panes at the pointer's location. Both panes will feature a vertical scroll bar.

Split a worksheet vertical into two panes

1 Click the split box to the right of the horizontal scroll bar. The cursor will turn into a double-arrow.

2 Holding down the mouse button, drag to the left until you reach the column at which you want to divide the worksheet. A grey dividing line shows where the window will be split.

3 Release the mouse button to divide the window into two panes at the pointer's location. Both panes will feature a horizontal scroll bar.

You can make the panes disappear by double-clicking anywhere on the split bar that divides the window.

Tip

Instead of using the split bars, you can divide a worksheet window by clicking the **Split** button on the **View** tab. This splits the worksheet window based on the position of a selected cell – the window is split vertically from the left edge of the cell and horizontally from the top edge. To remove the panes simply click **Split** again.

Sort data

By using Excel's Sort commands, you can make more sense of
the spreadsheet data by changing the order in which it appears.
For example, if you're creating a guest list for a birthday or
anniversary party, you can sort the guests by name alphabetically.

Sort data alphabetically

1 Select a cell in the column you want to sort (in this case, B).

2 On the **Data** tab, in the 'Sort & Filter' group, click the ascending
command sort **Sort A to Z**. If you want to see them in the
opposite order, click the descending command sort **Sort Z to A**.

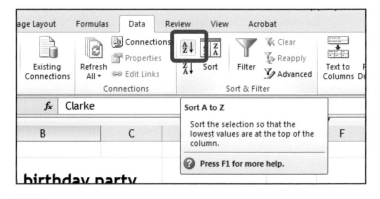

3 Your data will now be organised alphabetically.

Tip

Excel's 'Sort' command changes
to display either 'Sort A to Z'/'Sort
Smallest to Largest' options
depending on the type of data
selected in your spreadsheet.
If the data has a value, i.e. it is a
number, Excel offers the option
to sort it from smallest to largest
or vice versa. If you have text
selected, it will offer the option to
sort alphabetically instead.

Sort data numerically

1 Select a cell in the column you want to sort.

2 On the **Data** tab, in the 'Sort & Filter' group, click either the ascending command sort **Sort Smallest to Largest**, or the descending command sort **Sort Largest to Smallest**.

3 Your data will now be organised numerically.

Sort by date or time

1 Select a cell in the column you want to sort.

2 On the **Data** tab, in the 'Sort & Filter' group, click either the ascending command **Sort Oldest to Newest**, or the descending command **Sort Newest to Oldest**.

	File	Home	Insert	Page Layout	Formulas	Data	Review	View

Sort Oldest to Newest

Sort the selection so that the lowest values are at the top of the column.

❓ Press F1 for more help.

C5	fx	28/01/1974

	B	C	D
1			
2	0th birthday party		
3			
4	Surname	Birthday	
5	Clarke	28/01/1974	
6	Muller	07/02/1963	
7	Graves	22/06/1975	
8	Thompson	12/11/1969	
9	Farelly	27/08/1969	
10	Bertrand	25/10/1964	
11	Evans	18/12/1967	
12	Davis	03/07/1966	
13	Evans	14/06/1978	

3 Your data will now be organised by date or time.

Sort by cell colour, font colour or cell icon

1 On the **Data** tab, in the 'Sort & Filter' group, click **Sort**.

2 In the 'Sort' dialog box, click the **drop-down arrow** in the 'Column' field and select the column you want to 'Sort by'.

3 Click the **drop-down arrow** in the 'Sort On' field and select the value you want to sort by – either **Values**, **Cell Color**, **Font Color** or **Cell Icon**.

4 In the 'Order' field, click the **drop-down arrow** to choose a colour, then select whether you want it ordered **On Top** or **On Bottom**.

5 Click **OK**. The data will be now sorted by the formatting attributes you've chosen.

Customise your sorting

You can create your own sorting order using a Custom List. So, for example, in a wedding or party list, you could sort guests by their dietary requirements.

 Select the data you wish to sort.

2 On the **Data** tab, click **Sort** to open the 'Sort' dialog box.

3 Click the 'Column' field **drop-down arrow** and then select the column you want to sort. In this example, **Dietary**.

4 Make sure 'Values' is selected in the 'Sort On' field.

5 Click the 'Order' field **drop-down arrow** and choose **Custom List...**.

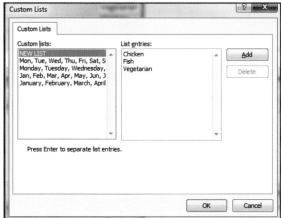

6 In the 'Custom Lists' dialog box select **NEW LIST**, and enter how you want your data sorted in the 'List entries' box. Here, the guests' dietary requirements are described as 'Chicken', 'Fish', 'Vegetarian'.

	A	B	C	D
2	**Mike's 50th birthday party**			
3				
4	**First Name**	**Surname**	**Attending**	**Dietary**
5	David	Bertrand	Yes	Chicken
6	Sandra	Brown	Yes	Chicken
7	Hugh	Clarke	Yes	Chicken
8	Anna	Clarkson	Yes	Chicken
9	Sam	Eastwood	Yes	Chicken
10	Andy	Evans	Yes	Chicken
11	Andrew	Blunt	Yes	Fish
12	Joseph	Clarke	Yes	Fish
13	Pete	Davis	Yes	Fish
14	June	Evans	Yes	Fish
15	Nina	Farelly	Yes	Fish
16	Linda	Farelly	Yes	Fish
17	Bridget	Fuller	Yes	Fish
18	Carmel	Hall	Yes	Fish
19	Samantha	Jones	Yes	Fish
20	Clive	Bertrand	Yes	Vegetarian
21	Jonathan	Graves	Yes	Vegetarian

Sheet1 Sheet2 Sheet3

Ready

7 Click **Add** to save the list, then click **OK**.

8 Click **OK** to close the 'Sort' dialog box and sort your data.

9 The spreadsheet will be sorted in order of 'Chicken', 'Fish' and 'Vegetarian' options.

Sort by more than one column or row

As part of Excel's custom sorting options, you can choose which columns to sort by and when by using multiple levels. This gives you more control over how your information is organised. In this example, data is sorted to show a number of teams within a league along with their team members.

Add a level

1 Select a cell and on the **Data** tab, in the 'Sort & Filter' group, click **Sort**.

2 In the 'Sort' dialog box, select the first item to 'Sort by'. In this example, Team names will be sorted from A to Z.

Sort					? X
⊕↓Add Level	✕ Delete Level	🗐 Copy Level	▲ ▼	Options...	☑ My data has headers
Column		Sort On		Order	
Sort by	Team	Values		A to Z	
	First Name				
	Surname				
	Birthday				
				OK	Cancel

3 Click **Add Level** to add another item.

4 Select the item you want to sort by next. Here, it is team members sorted from A to Z by their surname.

5 Click **OK**.

6 The data will be sorted so that teams are listed in order alphabetically, and within each team, its team members are listed alphabetically by last name.

Change sorting priority

1 On the **Data** tab, in the 'Sort & Filter' group, click **Sort**.

2 In the 'Sort' dialog box, select the level to be reordered by clicking on it (in this case the top Team level).

3 Click the **Move Up** or **Move Down arrows** to reorder the level. The higher the level is on the list, the higher its priority.

4 Click **OK**.

Use filters to quickly find data

Excel is very useful for compiling lots of data but when a worksheet grows very large with dozens of rows and columns, finding specific information can be a challenge. Filters can help by displaying only part of your data and hiding the rest from view. For example, you can filter an inventory list to view only those items that cost a certain price or are in the same category.

Filtering doesn't change your data in any way. When you remove the filter, all your data reappears exactly as it was before.

Add a filter

1 Check that your worksheet has a header row that identifies each column and that the data in each column is the same type. For example, don't mix text with numbers, or numbers with dates.

Inventory ID	Item type	Description	Unit Price	Quantity in Stock	Reorder Time in Days
AWT123	Clothing	Gents White Bowling Trousers	£40.99	15	14
AGT234	Clothing	Gents Grey Bowling Trousers	£48.99	10	14
BLZ765	Clothing	Ladies Blazer	£40.99	5	5
BLZ236	Clothing	Gents Blazer	£40.99	6	5
LWT987	Clothing	Ladies White Bowling Trousers	£30.99	10	5
LGT765	Clothing	Ladies Grey Bowling Trousers	£28.99	10	5
UVP675	Clothing	Unisex V-neck pullover	£21.99	6	10
UWJ239	Clothing	Unisex Waterproof Jacket	£49.99	7	5
SSB779	Clothing	Ladies Short Sleeve Blouse	£12.99	8	10
LWT569	Clothing	Ladies Waistcoat	£17.99	3	5
UPS453	Clothing	Unisex Polo Shirt	£9.99	9	5
BB3498	Misc	Bowls bag	£59.99	3	10
AWT123	Misc	Carry bag	£49.99	3	14
AGT234	Clothing	Gents Waistcoat	£17.99	10	5
BLZ765	Clothing	Ladies Waterproof jacket	£49.99	5	5
BLZ236	Clothing	Gents Waterproof jacket	£49.99	5	5
LWT987	Clothing	Ladies Match skirt	£20.99	7	5
LGT765	Clothing	Ladies Non-match skirt	£15.99	12	5
UVP675	Headwear	Gents white hat	£5.99	6	10
UWJ239	Headwear	Ladies white hat	£5.99	7	10
SSB779	Headwear	Gents trilby	£12.99	4	10
LWT569	Headwear	Ladies Hat	£15.99	6	10
UPS453	Misc	Score set	£4.99	11	14
BB3498	Misc	Small Silver trophy	£8.99	8	10

2 Click inside a worksheet, and then on the **Data** tab, in the 'Sort & Filter' group, click **Filter**. Filter arrows will appear next to each column heading.

3 Click the **filter arrow** for the column you want to filter (in this case, column F, 'Reorder Time in Days'). The 'Filter' menu appears.

4 Remove the check mark from **Select All**.

5 Select the check box for the data you want to view. Select multiple check boxes to see two or more items. In this example, the data will be filtered to show only those items that take 10 days to restock.

6 Click **OK**. All other data will be filtered, or temporarily hidden.

Add another filter

You can apply filters to multiple columns in a worksheet. Simply repeat Steps 3–6 on page 123 and above to apply filters to other columns. Filters are additive – you can use as many as necessary to narrow down your results. They are applied progressively, in the order you apply them. So each filter limits the data to which you can apply the next filter.

The example below shows how multiple filters can narrow your data. The worksheet has already been filtered to show only those items with a reorder time of 10 days. To display only the items that are in the category Misc in the 'Item type' column:

1 Click the **filter arrow** for the column you wish to filter. In this example, the **Item Type** column.

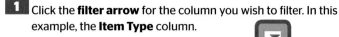

2 **Uncheck** the boxes next to the data you don't want to view. In this case, only the check box next to Misc is selected.

3 Click **OK**. In addition to the original filter, the new filter is applied, showing just the narrow range of data requested.

Remove a filter

1 Click the **filter arrow** in the column from which you want to clear the filter (in this case, 'Reorder Time in Days').

2 Choose **Clear Filter From...**.

3 The filter will be removed and the data that was previously hidden will be shown again.

Remove all the filters

1 To remove all filters in a worksheet, on the **Data** tab, in the 'Sort & Filter' group, click **Filter**.

2 The filters will be removed and all the data in the worksheet will be shown.

Advanced filtering

Excel lets you to perform more intricate types of filtering that can help you find the exact information you need from large amounts of data.

Filter using 'Search'

Instead of checking or unchecking entries in a filtered column list, you can search for data that contains an exact phrase, number or date, or a fragment of these. For example, searching for the exact phrase 'Gents' will display only items whose description contains that phrase.

1 On the **Data** tab, in the 'Sort & Filter' group, click **Filter**.

2 Click the **filter arrow** in the column you would like to filter (in this case, the 'Description' column).

3 In the drop-down menu, type in the data you want to see in the 'Search' box. The search results will appear automatically.

4 Tick the boxes next to the data you want to show and click **OK**. The worksheet will be filtered according to the search term.

Use advanced text filters

Using Excel's advanced text filter you can customise the data shown. For example, you can specify that only cells that contain a certain number of characters, or a certain word are shown.

1 On the **Data** tab, in the 'Sort & Filter' group, click **Filter**.

2 Click the **filter arrow** in the column of text that you want to filter (in this case, the 'Description' column).

3 From the drop-down menu, select **Text Filters** and then a filter, such as **Contains**....

4 In the 'Custom AutoFilter' dialog box, to the right of the filter, enter text you want to use (in this example, 'jacket') to view only cells that contain this text.

5 Click **OK**. The data will be filtered according to the filter and the text specified.

Use advanced number filters

With number filters you can view the numbered data in your worksheet in a myriad of ways. For example, in an inventory list you could display only those items that cost above or below a certain price, or those that fall within a specified range.

 On the **Data** tab, in the 'Sort & Filter' group, click **Filter**.

2 Click the **filter arrow** in the column of numbers that you want to filter (in this case, the 'Unit Price' column).

3 From the drop-down menu, select **Number Filters**.

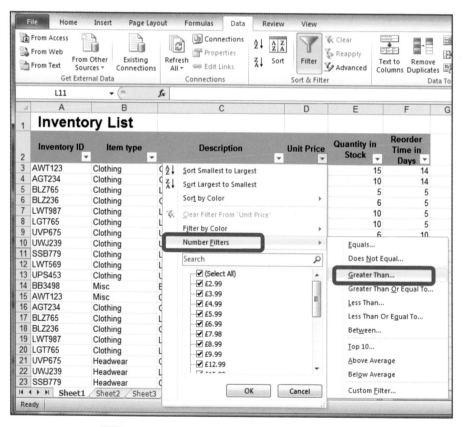

4 Select a filter, such as **Greater Than....**

5 In the 'Custom AutoFilter' dialog box, enter a number to the right of the filter field (in this case, items priced above £30).

6 Click **OK**. The data will be filtered according to the filter and the numbers you specified.

Use advanced date filters

Use these filters to display data from a certain time period, such as a specific year or between two dates.

1 On the **Data** tab, in the 'Sort & Filter' group, click **Filter**.

2 Click the **filter arrow** in the column of dates that you want to filter.

3 From the drop-down menu, select **Date Filters**.

4 Select a **filter**.

5 The worksheet will be filtered according to the date filter you chose.

Format your data as a table

To make working with your spreadsheet data as simple as possible, you can format it as a table.

Format data as a table

 Select the cells you want in the table.

2 On the **Home** tab, in the 'Styles' group, click **Format as Table**.

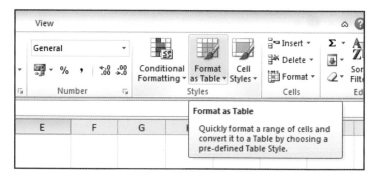

3 Select a table style from the list of predefined table styles.

4 A dialog box will appear, confirming the range of cells you've selected. You can change the range here by selecting a new range of cells directly on your spreadsheet.

Format As Table   ?   X

Where is the data for your table?

=$A$2:$E$31

☑ My table has headers

OK   Cancel

5 If your table has headers, check the box next to 'My table has headers'.

6 Click **OK**. The data will be formatted as a table in the style that you chose.

Add rows or columns to a table

1 Select any cell in your table.

2 On the **Design** tab, in the 'Properties' group, click **Resize Table**.

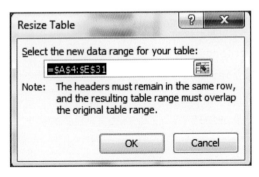

Resize Table   ?   X

Select the new data range for your table:

=$A$4:$E$31

Note: The headers must remain in the same row, and the resulting table range must overlap the original table range.

OK   Cancel

3 On your worksheet, select the new range of cells that you want to include – be sure to include the original table cells as well.

4 Click **OK** and the new rows and/or columns will be added to your table.

Change the table style

1 Select any cell in your table.

2 On the **Design** tab, in the 'Table Styles' group, click the **More drop-down arrow** to see all of the table styles.

3 Move the cursor over a style to see a live preview.

4 Select a style. Your table will change accordingly.

Tables include filtering by default. You can filter your data using the drop-down arrows in the header.

Change the Table Style Options

On the **Design** tab, there are six 'Table Style Options' that you can turn on or off to change a table's appearance: 'Header Row', 'Total Row', 'Banded Rows', 'First Column', 'Last Column' and 'Banded Columns'. Depending on the table style you are using, these options can have different effects, so you may need to experiment to achieve the look you're after.

Tip

To convert a table back into ordinary cells, in the 'Tools' group, click the Convert to Range command. The filters and the 'Design' tab will then disappear, but the cells will retain their data and formatting.

Get started with pivot tables

A pivot table is a special type of table that summarises data so that it's easier to understand. You can quickly change how Excel presents the summarised data in a pivot table by rearranging, hiding and displaying different category fields. Pivot tables help make sense of large amounts of information on a worksheet, making it easier to answer specific questions or gain new insights.

Create a pivot table

1 Select the table or cells containing the data you want to use. Make sure each column has a header and that there are no blank rows or columns.

2 On the **Insert** tab, in the 'Tables' group, click **PivotTable** to open the 'Create PivotTable' dialog box.

Month	Salesperson	Region	Product	Customer ID	Order amount
January	Jones, Sally	East Midlands	Apple Cider	29386	£ 925.00
February	Jones, Sally	South East	Apple Cider	74380	£ 875.00
March	Jones, Sally	West Midlands	Pear Cider	13452	£ 400.00
January	Clifton, Bill	South West	Apple Cider	41867	£ 1,500.00
February	Clifton, Bill	South East	Pear Cider	85769	£ 2,000.00
March	Clifton, Bill	West Midlands	Apple Cider	97831	£ 875.00
January	Davies, John	South East	Apple Cider	78452	£ 789.00
February	Davies, John	West Midlands	Apple Cider	90067	£ 545.00
March	Davies, John	South West	Apple Cider	52078	£ 605.00
January	Peterson, Ted	East Midlands	Apple Cider	34002	£ 1,045.00
February	Peterson, Ted	South East	Pear Cider	29004	£ 785.00
March	Peterson, Ted	South West	Pear Cider	37645	£ 560.00
January	Spelson, Caroline	South East	Apple Cider	70067	£ 2,400.00
February	Spelson, Caroline	South West	Apple Cider	67500	£ 1,400.00
March	Spelson, Caroline	East Midlands	Pear Cider	34987	£ 990.00
January	Halls, Tony	West Midlands	Pear Cider	13890	£ 790.00
February	Halls, Tony	South West	Apple Cider	21780	£ 1,200.00
March	Halls, Tony	South East	Apple Cider	45078	£ 1,570.00
January	Smith, Clive	East Midlands	Pear Cider	34605	£ 990.00

3 If necessary, adjust the range in the 'Table/Range' text box under the 'Select a table or range' option button.

4 Select a location for the pivot table. By default Excel places the pivot table in the existing worksheet but it's usually easier to work with when placed on a new worksheet.

5 Click **OK**.

6 A blank PivotTable will appear on the left, and a 'PivotTable Field List' task pane will appear on the right.

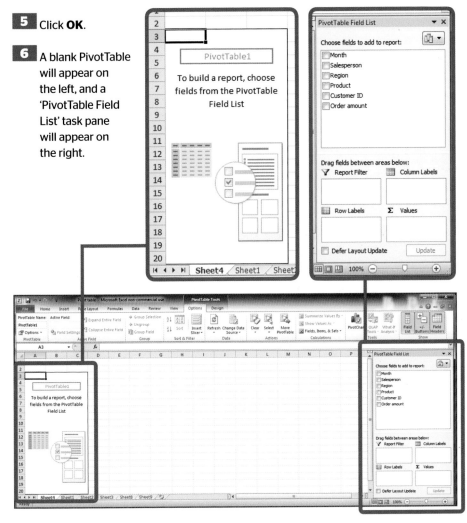

Assemble the pivot table

Next you need to assign fields in the 'PivotTable Field List' task pane to the various parts of the table. The task pane is divided into two areas: the 'Choose Fields to add to report' box with the names of all the fields (column headers in the source data) and an area below that's divided into four boxes:

■ **Report Filter:** add fields here to filter out sets of data. So, for example, if you select 'Salesperson' as a 'Report Filter' (see page 140), the pivot table will show data summaries for individual salespeople or for all.

■ **Column Labels:** add fields here to determine the data shown in the columns of the pivot table.

■ **Row Labels:** add fields here to determine the data shown in the rows of the pivot table.

■ **Values:** add fields here to determine the data shown in the pivot table's cells. These values are totalled in the pivot table's final column.

Add fields

1 In the 'Choose fields to add to report' list in the 'Pivot Table Field List', tick each field you want to add.

PivotTable Field List

Choose fields to add to report:

- [ ] Month
- [x] **Salesperson**
- [ ] Region
- [ ] Product
- [ ] Customer ID
- [x] **Order amount**

2 Drag a field name from the ticked 'Choose Fields to add to report' list box and drop it in one of the four areas below. In this example, the 'Salesperson' field is added to the 'Row Labels' area, and the 'Order amount' is added to the 'Values' area.

3 The PivotTable now shows the data according to the fields selected – in this example, the amount sold in each region.

Drag fields between areas below:

▼ Report Filter   ▦ Column Labels

▦ Row Labels   Σ Values

Region   ▼   Sum of Order... ▼

☐ Defer Layout Update   Update

▦ ▢ ▥ 100% ⊖ ───────── ⊕

Row Labels	▾	Sum of Order amount
East Midlands	£	5,960.00
South East	£	11,279.00
South East	£	785.00
South West	£	8,855.00
West Midlands	£	3,480.00
Grand Total	**£**	**30,359.00**

4 Add or change fields in each box to see different results. For example, in this pivot table, the columns can be changed to see how many items were sold by region.

Add column labels

To show multiple columns, you need to add Column Labels.

 Drag a field (for example, 'Month') from the 'Field List' into the 'Column Labels' area.

2 The PivotTable will now have multiple columns. In this example, there is a column for each month, and the PivotTable shows the total order amount for each month as well as each salesperson's total sales for the three months listed.

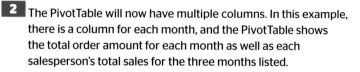

Row Labels	January	February	March	Grand Total
Spelson, Caroline	2400	1400	990	4790
White, Sarah	2010	1560	1200	4770
Clifton, Bill	1500	2000	875	4375
Halls, Tony	790	1200	1570	3560
Smith, Clive	990	1345	1090	3425
Walker, Jack	870	995	1045	2910
Peterson, Ted	1045	785	560	2390
Jones, Sally	925	875	400	2200
Davies, John	789	545	605	1939
Grand Total	11319	10705	8335	30359

As with ordinary data, you can apply any type of formatting to a pivot table cell. For example, you may want to change the 'Number Format' to 'Accounting' (see pages 49–54).

Do more with pivot tables

Once you've mastered the art of creating pivot tables, you can then use filters and slicers, along with sorting column values, to explore your data in more detail.

Sort a pivot table

You can reorder the values in a PivotTable by sorting on one or more of its Column or Row fields.

1 Click the filter button for the 'Row Labels' field you want to sort.

2 From the drop-down menu click either:

■ **Sort A to Z:** to sort alphabetically, numeric values from the smallest to largest, or dates from the oldest to newest.

■ **Sort Z to A:** to sort in reverse alphabetical order, numeric values from the largest to smallest, or dates from the newest to oldest.

3 Click **OK**.

4 To sort the Column fields, select a cell in the column you want to sort and then on the **Options** tab click **Sort**. In the 'Sort By Value'

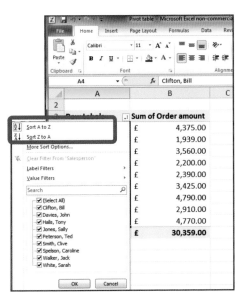

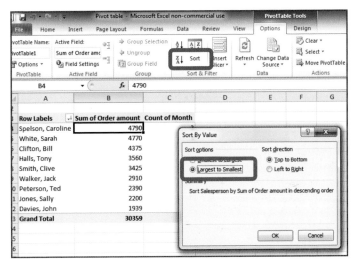

dialog box, select a sort option (in this example, **Largest to Smallest**). Then click **OK** to see the values in the column ordered as you've just specified.

Add a report filter

You can filter the data in an Excel 2010 pivot table in order to focus on just part of the data. You do this by adding a field to the 'Report Filter' area. Then you can use the filter button on the pivot table to select an option from the drop-down menu to display only the summary data for that subset.

1 Drag a field from the 'Field List' into the 'Report Filter' area (in this case, the 'Salesperson' field).

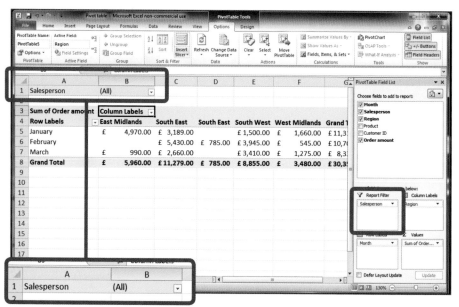

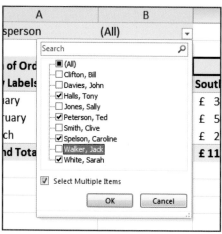

2 The report filter appears above the PivotTable. Click the **drop-down arrow** to the right of the filter to see the list of items.

3 Select the item that you wish to view. To select more than one item, place a checkmark next to 'Select Multiple Items'. Then click **OK**. In this example, four salespeople have been selected.

4 Click **OK**. The PivotTable adjusts to reflect the changes.

Add a slicer

A new feature of Excel 2010, slicers offer a quick and easy way to filter your pivot table. Slicers work in the same way as report filters, but they're more interactive and faster to use so you can see results instantly.

 Select any cell in your PivotTable.

2 On the **Options** tab, click **Insert Slicer**. In the resulting dialog box select the desired field. Then click **OK**.

Do more with pivot tables

Tip
You can create a PivotChart from your PivotTable. As with regular charts (see pages 142-6), you can choose a chart type, layout and style. To create a PivotChart, click any cell in the PivotTable. On the **Options** tab, click **PivotChart** and select a chart type. The PivotChart will appear in the worksheet.

3 The slicer appears next to the PivotTable. Select or deselect items – the PivotTable will instantly update to reflect the changes. Each selected item is highlighted in blue, and only the selected items are displayed in the PivotTable. To select more than one item, hold down the **Ctrl** key and then click on each item or, if the items are adjacent, you can select by clicking and dragging the mouse.

nds	Grand Total
.00	£ 4,004.00
.00	£ 4,620.00
.00	£ 3,450.00
.00	£ 12,074.00

Salesperson

- Clifton, Bill
- Davies, John
- Halls, Tony
- Jones, Sally
- Peterson, Ted
- Smith, Clive
- Spelson, Caroline
- Walker, Jack

Work with charts

Displaying data graphically as a chart can make it easier to understand and analyse. Excel comes with many different types of charts, including columns, line and pie charts, so you can choose one that displays your data to best effect. You can even create a combination chart by using more than one chart type at a time.

Create a chart

1 Select the cells that you want to chart, including the column titles and the row labels. The content of these cells will provide the source data for the chart.

2 On the **Insert** tab, in the 'Charts' group, click a chart category such as 'Column'.

File	Home	Insert	Page Layout	Formulas	Data	Review	View

PivotTable Table | Picture Clip Art | Shapes ▾ SmartArt Screenshot ▾ | Column | Line ▾ Area ▾ Pie ▾ Scatter ▾ Bar ▾ Other Charts ▾

Tables | Illustrations | Charts

	A1	▾	f_x	TEAM

Column

Insert a column chart.

Column charts are used to compare values across categories.

	A	B	C
1	TEAM	WINS	LOSS
2			
3	South Mimms	9	1
4	Hatfield North	8	2
5	Hatfield South	5	5
6	Welwyn South	2	8
7	Digswell	2	8
8	Stevenage	1	9
9	Hertford	3	7
10	St Albans	7	3
11	Radlett	6	4
12			
13			
14			
15			
16			
17			

3 Select a chart type from the drop-down menu.

4 The chart will appear in the worksheet.

Switch row and column data

When creating a chart, the worksheet data may not be grouped the way you need it to be. For example, you want a column chart to illustrate, say, monthly club membership revenue, but prefer to show the month on the horizontal axis rather than on the vertical axis as generated by Excel. Fortunately, you can swap row and column data after you've created your chart.

1 Select the existing chart by clicking on it.

2 On the **Design** tab, in the 'Data' group, select **Switch Row/ Column**.

3 The chart will readjust.

Change the chart type

1 From the **Design** tab, in the 'Type' group, click **Change Chart Type**. A dialog box appears.

2 Click a chart type.

3 Click **OK**.

Change the chart layout

1 On the **Design** tab, in the 'Chart Layouts' group, click the **More drop-down arrow** to see all of the chart layouts.

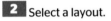

2 Select a layout.

3 The chart will update to reflect the new layout.

Change the chart style

1 On the **Design** tab, in the 'Chart Styles' group, click the **More drop-down arrow** to see all available styles.

2 Click a style.

3 The chart will update to reflect the new style.

Tip

Neither the 'Chart Layout' nor the 'Chart Styles' galleries offer a live preview. This means that you have to click a thumbnail from the gallery and apply it to the chart in order to see how it looks.

Move a chart to a different worksheet

When you create a chart, it's automatically embedded on the same worksheet as the source data, but you may prefer to move it onto its own worksheet to make it easier to work with.

1 On the **Design** tab, in the 'Location' group, click **Move Chart**.

2 In the 'Move Chart' dialog box, the current location of the chart is shown. Select a new location for the chart.

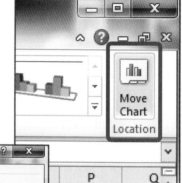

Move Chart

Choose where you want the chart to be placed:

○ New sheet: Chart1

● Object in: Sheet2

OK   Cancel

3 Click **OK**. The chart will appear in the new location.

4 If you later decide to move the chart back to the same worksheet as the data it represents, click **Move Chart** on the **Design** tab again and this time click the **Object In** button. Select the name of the worksheet from the drop-down menu, then click **OK**.

Tip
Once you've created a chart, it's easy to move or resize it. To move it, click with the mouse inside the chart and drag the chart to a new location. To resize, move the mouse over one of the selection handles. When the pointer changes to a double-headed arrow, drag the side or corner to enlarge or reduce the chart.

Get started with sparkline graphics

Sparklines are miniature charts that fit into a single cell. Unlike a chart, a sparkline is usually adjacent to the data, so it can help bring immediate meaning and context to numbers. They are particularly good for showing trends and patterns.

There are three types of sparklines: 'Line', 'Column' and 'Win/Loss' and you find them on the **Insert** tab.

'Line' and 'Column' are similar to line and column charts, while 'Win/Loss' sparklines show whether each value is positive or negative, rather than how high or low it is. All three can display markers at key points, such as the highest and lowest points, which makes them easier to read.

Create sparklines

In this example, sparklines are created to illustrate the progress of a team in a local competition. As with formulas, create a single sparkline first and then use the fill handle to automatically create the sparklines for the remaining rows.

1 Select an empty cell or group of empty cells where you want to show your sparkline.

2 On the **Insert** tab, in the 'Sparklines' group, click the type of sparkline that you want to create: **Line**, **Column** or **Win/Loss**. In this case, 'Line'.

3 In the 'Create Sparklines' dialog box, type the range of the cells that contain the data on which you want to base the sparklines in the 'Data Range' box. Alternatively, click and drag on the worksheet with your cursor to select the data range. This will automatically fill the data range.

Create Sparklines

Choose the data that you want

Data Range: B3:G3

Choose where you want the sparklines to be placed

Location Range: $H$3

OK   Cancel

4 Click **OK**. The sparkline will appear in the document.

	A	B	C	D	E	F	G	H	I
1	TEAM	week1	week2	week3	week4	week5	week6		
2									
3	South Mimms	1	1	1	1	1	0		
4	Hatfield North	1	0	1	1	1	0		
5	Hatfield South	0	0	1	1	1	1		
6	Welwyn South	1	0	1	0	0	0		
7	Digswell	0	0	0	0	1	1		
8	Stevenage	0	1	0	0	0	1		
9	Hertford	1	1	1	0	0	0		
10	St Albans	0	1	0	1	0	0		
11	Radlett	0	0	0	1	0	1		
12	Cheshunt	1	1	0	0	1	1		
13									
14									
15									
16									
17									
18									

Sparkline Tools — Design

File   Home   Insert   Page Layout   Formulas   Data   Review   View   Design

Edit Data ▾   Line   Column   Win/Loss   □ High Point   □ First Point   □ Low Point   □ Last Point   □ Negative Points   ✓ Markers

Sparkline   Type   Show

H3

5 Click and drag the fill handle downward.

6 Sparklines will be created for the remaining rows.

Change the sparkline style

1 Select the sparklines that you want to change.

2 On the **Design** tab, in the 'Style' group, click the **More drop-down arrow** to show all of the available styles.

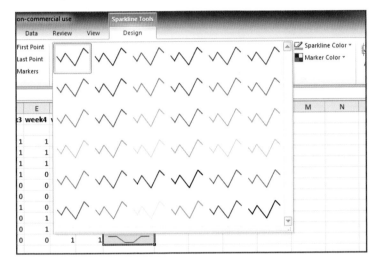

3 Click a style.

4 The sparklines will update to show the selected style.

Show points on the sparkline
You can emphasise certain points on the sparkline with markers or dots – helping to add meaning to the chart.

1 Select the sparklines that you want to change.

2 On the **Design** tab, in the 'Show' group, tick the check box of the points you want to illustrate.

3 To change the colour of the dots, on the **Design** tab, click on **Marker Color** and select a colour for each type of marker you're using.

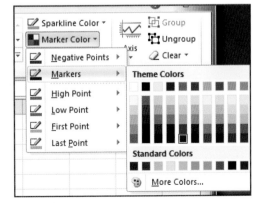

Change the display range

In order to fill the whole cell, each sparkline is scaled to fit the maximum and minimum values of its own data. However, when you're comparing several sparklines, it's not clear at a glance which ones have higher or lower values. You can get round this problem by making the display range the same for all of the sparklines.

1 Select the sparklines that you want to change.

2 On the **Design** tab, click **Axis**.

3 From the drop-down menu, under 'Vertical Axis Minimum Value Options' and 'Vertical Axis Maximum Value Options', select **Same for All Sparklines**.

4 The sparklines will update to reflect the new range.

Tip

You can control how Excel displays empty cells in the sparkline graphic using the 'Hidden and Empty Cell Setting' dialog box. To access this, on the **Design** tab, in the 'Sparkline' group, click **Edit Data**. Then click **Hidden & Empty Cells** and in the dialog box that appears click **Gaps**, **Zero** or **Connect data points with line**. Click **OK** to exit.

Resources

Keyboard shortcuts

Press these keys	To do this
Ctrl + N	Create a new workbook
Ctrl + O	Open a workbook
Ctrl + S	Save the active workbook with its current file name and location
Ctrl + P	Print a workbook
Ctrl + W	Close the selected workbook window
Ctrl + A	Select the entire worksheet
Ctrl + Z	Undo the last action
Ctrl + C	Copy the selected cells
Ctrl + X	Cut the selected cells
Ctrl + V	Paste copied cells
Ctrl + L	Display the 'Create Table' dialog box
Ctrl + B	Apply or remove bold formatting
Ctrl + I	Apply or remove italic formatting
Ctrl + H	Display the 'Find and Replace' dialog box
Shift + F11	Insert a new worksheet in the current workbook
Ctrl + Page Down	Move to the next worksheet in the current workbook
Ctrl + Page Up	Move to the previous worksheet in the current workbook
Tab	Move left to right, cell by cell
Shift + Tab	Move right to left, cell by cell
Enter	Move down, cell by cell
Shift + Enter	Move up, cell by cell
Ctrl + Shift + Down Arrow or Up Arrow	Move down or up to the last empty or non-empty cell
Ctrl + Shift + Right Arrow or Left Arrow	Move to the last empty or non-empty cell to the right or left
Backspace	Delete data in the current cell
Alt + Enter	Insert a return within a cell
Ctrl + Page Down	Go to the next workstation
Ctrl + Page Up	Go to the previous worksheet
Ctrl + ;	Enter the current date
Ctrl + 1	Display the 'Format Cells' dialog box
Alt + F1	Create a chart of the selected data

Jargon buster

AutoComplete Automatically duplicates the entries in a worksheet column in subsequent rows whenever you start a new entry that begins with the same letter or letters as an existing entry in that column.

AutoCorrect Automatically corrects spelling or replaces text with pre-specified entries.

AutoFill Automatically fills cells with preset data, such as months of the year and days of the week. You can add your own custom AutoFill series.

Backstage view Set of commands accessible from the green File tab, which let you save, manage and view the properties of the workbook file you're editing.

Cell The intersection of a column and row in the worksheet.

Cell reference Refers to a particular cell or range of cells in your worksheet.

Clip art Ready-made artwork that's included with Word or downloaded from the web for use in your documents.

Compatibility Checker A utility that alerts you to potential compatibility issues if you plan to save an Excel workbook file in the older Excel 97-2003 file format.

Conditional formatting The ability to change the appearance of cell data if certain conditions - which you can specify - are met.

Current cell The cell that contains the cursor. Always described as active - only one cell per worksheet can be current or active at any time.

Dialog box A window that pops up to display or request information.

Dialog box launcher A small icon in the lower-right corner of a group of commands on the Ribbon that you click to open a dialog box with further settings and commands.

Digital signature An electronic, encrypted, stamp of authentication used on digital files such as documents or email messages. A digital signature confirms that the file originated from the signer and has not been altered.

Drop-down menu A list of options that appears when you click a menu name or button, usually marked with a down-pointing arrow.

Field An area or container on screen that holds information.

File format Refers to the specific way that information is stored within a computer file. The letters that appear after the file name show what type of file it is and what type of program will open it - for example, a Microsoft Excel file ends in .xlsx.

Fill handle A small black dot or square in the bottom right corner of the active cell that can be used to copy a cell's contents to adjacent cells.

Formula A mathematical equation entered into a cell that instructs Excel to perform a calculation.

Formula bar The horizontal toolbar located below the Ribbon that shows the cell reference and contents of the current cell. You can use it to enter or edit formulas and cell entries, and assign names to cells.

Function Part of a formula that works with a number of specific arguments and then returns a single value based on those arguments.

Gallery A drop-down list of thumbnail selections, which appears when you select specific commands on the Ribbon.

Mathermatical operator The symbols used to specify the type of calculation that you want the formula to perform. For example, the * (asterisk) operator multiplies numbers.

Name box The left-most area of the Formula bar that shows the reference or name of the current cell.

Pivot table A special type of table that lets you summarise large amounts of data, then pivot or rearrange the table's data to display different summaries of the information it contains.

Pop-up A small window that appears next to an item on screen to give additional information.

Quick Access toolbar A small toolbar to the right of the Office button that includes common commands, such as Save and Undo.

Saturation How rich the colours are in a digital image.

Scroll bars Horizontal and vertical bars at the bottom and right side of the worksheet window that let you quickly move to a different area of a worksheet.

Sharpness The clarity of detail in a photo.

Sizing handles When you click a shape, image or piece of clip art, a border with little white squares and circles will appear around it. These are the sizing handles. Click and drag on the squares to change the height or width, or on the circles to make the whole object smaller or bigger.

Slicer A new feature in Excel 2010 that lets you quickly filter the contents of a PivotTable on more than one field.

SmartArt graphics Pre-drawn diagrams and illustrations that can be inserted into your workbook. You can edit the diagrams and change the style without having to fiddle with shape size and alignment, as SmartArt graphics automatically adjust to maintain their overall shape and design.

Sparklines Tiny miniature charts that fit within a single cell. Used to illustrate basic trends in data.

Status bar A horizontal line of information shown at the bottom or top of a program window.

Text alignment Describes the position of text within cells.

WordArt Stylized text formatting for headings and other text in Excel 2007 worksheets.

Workbook The file that you create in Excel. A new workbook consists of three worksheets by default.

Worksheet The document that you work in when you enter data into cells within Excel. A worksheet is stored in a workbook.

Worksheet tabs Small tabs at the bottom of a worksheet window that you click to move between the worksheets in a workbook.

Resources